More Ki

More Kinds of Rugby

RAY FRENCH

THE KINGSWOOD PRESS

The Kingswood Press
an imprint of Methuen London
Michelin House, 81 Fulham Road, London SW3 6RB

First published 1989
ISBN 434 98179 6

All the illustrations in this book, on the cover (of Hugh Waddell, Jonathan Davies and Alan Tait) and inside, except for two, are reproduced by kind permission of Andrew Varley. The exceptions are numbered 2 and 3, and are from the author's private collection.

Printed and bound in Great Britain
by Richard Clay Ltd, Bungay, Suffolk

Contents

Author's Note

As this book was going to press, Mansfield Marksman changed its name to Nottingham City. There was just time to mark that change in two places in chapter 6. Elsewhere throughout the book I'm afraid I must crave the reader's indulgence wherever references to Mansfield Marksman occur.

R.F.

Introduction

Observers of the rugby scene in Britain in 1989, whether League or Union, might well be perplexed by what has been happening to their respective sports in the 1980s. If, like me, they have been, or are still, involved in playing, coaching or writing about both codes, or simply enjoy watching them, they will accept that many recent events, often totally contradictory to previous attitudes firmly held by either code, could not have taken place before. I am not entirely sure that the governing bodies of either code really realise just how fundamental some of the changes are that are taking place in their midst. But let us glance at some of the more perplexing.

Of course, some that have kindled my interest have also, not surprisingly, commanded the attention of the media; others, more personal, have simply aroused my curiosity and strengthened my certainty of the directions in which both codes of rugby are moving. For example, most sports lovers were outraged when the unfortunate Welsh Rugby Union winger, Steve Ford, the brother of Phil Ford, the Bradford Northern and Great Britain RL player, was banned from taking any further part in Rugby Union. His crime of playing a trial for Leeds RLFC, though without payment and with a view to judging simply whether or not he might be considered suitable for League, was sufficient to have him suspended *sine die*.

Within twelve months, however, the same sporting body that sought his ban, the Welsh RFU, fought for and won his reinstatement as a player within the Union code. A strange change of heart from a body whose record in the past over such incidents has been uncompromising, to say the least.

The progress made by amateur Rugby League in the south of England has been quite remarkable in recent seasons but eyebrows were raised when the 1988 London RL Cup final was played at the home of Wasps Rugby Union club, as it was again in 1989, and was also covered by BBC Radio.

Eyebrows were raised again when under-the-counter payments in the South African Rugby Union came into the open. Having been promised R6000 (about £1400 at the current rate of exchange) to play for the Welkom Club in 1986, Nelis van Rooyen took his club president to court when he received only a quarter of that amount; and the Transvaal rugby boss, Louis Luyt, admitted that his players had received R250 (about £60) a match throughout the season. Just before a game at Newlands in 1988, billed as a final Springbok trial, the country's leading players demanded appearance money and tore the sponsor's logo from their jerseys when their demands were refused. In May 1989, it was reported that the leading Currie Cup team, Western Province, had threatened to strike before their game against Northern Transvaal if their match fee was not increased. Western Province officials then confirmed that their players were given R700 (about £170) a game as 'expenses'. In New Zealand, in May 1989, the All Blacks' Grant Fox and the NZ committee member J. J. Stewart were quoted as saying that players should be allowed to retain whatever fees they might be paid for lending their name to advertising, especially on television, and that trust funds for players should now be allowed. Not surprisingly, the International Board have, so far, shown a distinct lack of interest in all these matters.

The International Board did, however, assert themselves in March 1985 to change the law under which, only six months before, I had been banned from my work with the Lancashire Schools Rugby Union committee, owing to my previous involvement in professional Rugby League. This welcome and immediate about-turn, in the face of hostile opposition from within the Union code itself, was much quicker than anyone could have expected and all the more curious for that. And yet, despite these occasional outbursts of apparent hostility, there have been increasing signs of a much greater awareness of, and understanding between, the rival rugby codes.

The sight of twenty-six students, all with strong Rugby Union backgrounds, representing Wales and Scotland in a universities Rugby League international at St Helens, and the playing of League and Union matches on parallel pitches on the same afternoon at my school and others like it, have been novel events to anyone such as myself who has been involved in the complex relations between both sports for the best part of thirty-five years.

But surely the most perplexing as well as the most amusing scene of the 1980s, and one which highlights more than any the change of outlook between the two codes, was the sight of the Hull KR coach, Roger Millward, discussing with the Pontypool captain and scrum-half, David Bishop, in the middle of the men's bar in the Waterloo RU club, the possibilities of Bishop signing professional forms for Hull KR. No longer for Roger Millward and his deputation of directors a discreet meeting behind the club house or in a shady bar far from the ground, but a welcome to the Waterloo bar and the freedom to chase their quarry undisturbed, save for banter between myself and a friendly Waterloo official who jokingly inquired whether his club would receive 10 per cent of any fee. Long gone are the days of the 1970s when

Alex Murphy was ejected from the Fylde Rugby Union clubhouse for trying to speak to a player. International players in the southern hemisphere now even send messages of goodwill to each other before millions of television viewers as when, commentating on the Rugby League World Cup match between New Zealand and Great Britain in Christchurch, New Zealand, I was surprised to hear my co-commentator, Tony Palmer, send the good wishes of the All Blacks Union side and their coach Alex Wyllie to the Kiwis League team.

Such incidents, many apparently unrelated, are examples of the sporting and social progress made by the League code in the 1980s and evidence of the two codes at last coming to terms with each other, often at the insistence of a more tolerant society and through the financial and sporting constraints now being forced upon them. When rugby historians look back at the past decade they might call it the Age of Enlightenment, when both games were forced to take a good look at their once entrenched positions and abandon policies which only a few years ago seemed destined to be enshrined in tablets of stone.

Having played both codes at club and international level and having been involved in the coaching and administration of both games, I find myself in possibly a unique position to assess the present strengths and weaknesses of each, and to guess at the outcome of today's changing attitudes. The more relaxed relationships within both governing bodies, and between players and supporters is, I believe, leading to a future which may spring considerable surprises for the entrenched followers of both camps. It will then be interesting to see whether it is League or Union that breasts the tape first as the major spectator sport in the twenty-first century or whether, as I suspect, both arrive at the tape together, somewhat out of breath, and with even the finest of judges having difficulty separating the one from the other.

1

Lessons From Overseas

By the late 1970s Rugby Union certainly commanded the respect of the sporting public, thanks largely to the success of the British Lions and their style of play in Test victories over South Africa and New Zealand. It was at that same time that many of us began to fear for the future of Rugby League. By the end of the 1976–77 season, the game was in danger of slipping quietly out of the public's consciousness and into a northern parochial backwater. The try-scoring charts for that season had been topped by Stuart Wright of Widnes with a mere 31 tries, the only player to pass the thirty mark. Attendances had declined, with gates passing 10,000 on only thirteen occasions and with only one match, apart from the challenge Cup final, attracting a crowd above 20,000. A sorry state of affairs, accelerated by the failure of many clubs to raise an A team, in which young talent could be developed. What a difference from the situation only ten years later – and with what optimism do we now look forward to the 1990s.

A fully sponsored Slalom Lager Alliance league of A teams from a record twenty-nine clubs is producing the youngsters needed to attract the crowds, now returning to the game in ever increasing numbers. In the 1986–87 season over forty-three matches enjoyed gates of over 10,000, seven over 20,000, and four above 30,000. The following season saw a further staggering increase in attendances with a 20 per cent increase in first division gates, the best average attendances since the re-introduction of two divisions sixteen years ago, and a 40 per cent increase within the second division. And on top of that a further 25 per cent increase was recorded in 1988–89.

These large crowds were at last seeing a feast of tries again when Ellery Hanley (Wigan) completed his tally for 1986–87 with no less than 63 to head the charts, while another five players exceeded 30. The following season saw the arrival of League's latest wing sensation, the former Rosslyn Park Rugby Union player, Martin Offiah, who topped the charts with 44 tries and continued his spectacular running with a further 19 on Great Britain's tour of Australasia in the summer of 1988. His exciting running alone almost doubled the gates at Widnes in what proved to be their championship season.

The arrival of David Oxley and David Howes in 1974 as the new secretary and public relations officer of the Rugby Football League have proved exceptional appointments, and since that time they and the League's other officers have presided over rule changes which have had an enormously stimulating effect on the game. The introduction of the differential penalty for technical offences at the scrum, the fostering of the six-tackle rule and the handover rule, whereby a team is forced to hand over possession to their opponents at the conclusion of six tackles, have all had their beneficial effect on the modern style of play. With less emphasis on forward battles of attrition in midfield, the need for greater standards of physical strength and fitness, and the more free flowing nature of the game, it is little wonder that the League code is proving so attractive in areas well outside its original confines.

In a personality conscious society, many of the code's leading players have attained a national status undreamed of a few years ago. The arrival of stars from Australia and New Zealand, after the ban on overseas players was lifted in 1984, has been tremendously important, and those players' skills, fitness, commitment, and thoroughly professional attitude to the game must be seen as one of the key factors in Rugby League's revival in this country.

Introduced at the close of the miserable 1976–77 season, the original ban on signing overseas players was an attempt to keep in this country, for the benefit of British spectators, such talents as Cliff Watson, Mal Reilly, Tommy Bishop, and John Gray all of whom were wanted by Australian clubs. Sadly, the ban had an adverse effect for it not only halted the ambitions of many home-based players but, more important, prevented overseas players, who have always played a particularly vibrant part in British Rugby League, from playing in this country. Thankfully wiser counsels prevailed in the end and the removal of the ban has not only brought overseas stars to Britain but has given British players the incentive to prove themselves good enough to play for Australian or New Zealand clubs during the British summer. Some of the world's greatest players are once again providing the glamour the British fans want to see. But little did I realise the headaches I would suffer in helping to secure their re-introduction . . .

'Mission accomplished' were my first words, 12,000 miles away across the globe, from my hotel room in Brisbane to the home of John Clegg, the chairman of St Helens RLFC on the night of 26 June 1984. That was enough to send the town into ecstasy as the news spread quickly through the Pilkington Glass Works and other local industries that the 6-foot, 16-stone Australian Test centre, the record points-scoring sensation of the 1982 Kangaroos tour, Mal Meninga, had signed for the Saints. But, clutching in my sweating hand the white registration form which tied the great player to St Helens, I wondered to myself, 'At what cost to my sanity?' I had a mental picture of the relief shown on Neville Chamberlain's face when he held that famous sheet of paper on his return from Munich. Would I too be so deluded? It was to be twelve months later, when the giant Meninga had restored the ailing St Helens club's fortunes by helping them to capture the Lancashire Cup and the Slalom Lager Premiership Trophy, before I could relax and assess the importance of what I had achieved.

Being an avid reader of spy stories, I always imagine the powers that be in MI5, when planning a foray by one of their agents into foreign territory, to meet in a secluded back room of some unpretentious building in London, ready for the briefing of their man. A firm handshake, fond farewells, a pat on the back and a quiet 'For Queen and Country', and off goes the agent into the night. Such was my introduction into what was termed, by one imaginative press man, as 'The great Australian Big Game Hunt', the only difference being that my briefing took place during a school lunch break in May in the back office of the St Helens club in the company of the Saints' head of secret operations, John Clegg, and his secretary, Geoff Sutcliffe. I received the blank registration forms, deposited them in my brief-case amid a thousand statistics already prepared for my task as BBC radio reporter on the forthcoming Great Britain tour of Australia and received the obligatory handshake and farewell message, 'For the town and the club, Ray'. I was out on my own, stalking my quarry, but with the knowledge that other agents were also in hot pursuit. How close they were to the quarry I only realised when I sat down to breakfast a week later in the Sheraton Hotel, Sydney with Joe Warham and Harry Jepson, the representatives of the Leeds club. My morning newspaper also told me that Maurice Lindsay, Wigan's diminutive but dynamic director, was already established on the Australian Gold Coast and hoping to strike in Brisbane. The hunt was truly on.

The relaxation of the ban on Anglo-Australian transfers had been the cause of this flurry of activity. But little did I realise the urgency of the situation as British clubs fought frantically to outbid each other in the Australian market. The attempt to lighten the gloom of many a northern wintry afternoon with a sprinkling of Antipodean star signings was at its height in that summer of 1984.

Breakfast that morning was to be a most upsetting one and possibly to prove the most embarrassing moment of my entire rugby career. I was distinctly put off my generous portion of bacon and eggs when Joe Warham and Harry Jepson, my good friends of many years standing, told me they were to meet with Mal Meninga in Brisbane and even asked me my opinion of his ability. Panic and embarrassment hit me at once, especially when Joe confirmed that the intrepid Maurice Lindsay was already hot on the trail of Australian green and gold. I knew I would be stuck in Sydney for the next two weeks to report on Great Britain's matches, and I was mortified at having to deceive Joe Warham. With hurried excuses for leaving my breakfast ('jet lag') and with my brain reeling, I raced upstairs to the sanctuary of my room and the telephone – my lifeline to success.

Having made a series of furtive telephone calls, under the name of a bogus English pressman, to the hotel headquarters where the Queensland team were in training, I finally persuaded Mal Meninga to sign nothing until I could meet him in a fortnight's time in Brisbane. To his credit he agreed and kept his word, as this most honest of gentle giants did throughout all our bargainings. But the strain of that next fortnight and the mental scars inflicted every time I read about Leeds and Meninga in daily press reports will live with me forever.

Thankfully, when I arrived with the Lions squad in Brisbane two weeks later, much of the groundwork carried out by the president of the Souths club, Tony Testa, and his friend at St Helens, John Clegg, paved the way for my secret meeting with Meninga, though in classic spy-film fashion other agents were lurking in the trees! Having arranged to be picked up at the Gazebo Hotel, Brisbane by the Souths coach Wayne Bennett I was deposited in the middle of the training pitch under the pretext that I was to watch a coaching session in the hope of learning a few tips which could be used in the preparation of my school teams at home. All went well with the ploy until Messrs Warham and Jepson emerged from the shadows of the clubhouse, obviously satisfied with their discussions with Meninga but inquisitive of what I was doing. I even took part in a coaching routine to throw them off the scent. I did. They left quietly but confident they had won the prize.

Deliberately clad in a St Helens past-players sweater and offering Mal Meninga a current Saints sweater I hoped to achieve a more relaxed attitude in our discussions, to present the image of a well satisfied ex-player encouraging a new player to embark upon a career at his old club. Over a lager in the Souths clubhouse my plan worked for we developed such an easy rapport that, never once looking at the contract which appeared from my back trouser pocket, Mal agreed to sign following the second Test at Lang Park on that fateful Tuesday evening 26 June. The slight delay would enable his solicitor to check the contract. A week of complete silence on both our parts followed amid mounting tension for me as press reports still insisted that Mal would be a Leeds player or that Wigan were closing in rapidly. None the less, to Mal's eternal credit and to my relief he kept his word. And there was no more nervous reporter who made his way after the second Test to the victorious dressing-room of the Australian side than I. I didn't want interviews, though; I only wanted a signature.

Being an ex-player, gifted with 16 stones and 6 foot 3 inches, enabled me to fight my way through the crowd to meet Mal in the corridor outside the Kangaroos dressing-room. The tension: would he or would he not sign? The time was 9.30 p.m. and I had arranged to telephone John Clegg at 11.30. I was within minutes of success or failure. The huge man came towards me, a kindly smile on his face, and I knew I had won. The registration form was duly placed on an upturned Foster's Lager box and I reached for my pen. I had *lost* it in the battle to enter the dressing-room! 'Why does this happen to me', I thought, as I raced round for another one. My literary training reminded me that tragedy can oft be found near comedy but this was not to be. With the forms duly signed, a welcoming handshake on behalf of St Helens, and within minutes a taxi was whisking me to make the longed-for call to the Saints' chairman.

Nor was the drama or comedy over even then for, following a rest on my hotel bed and a refreshing beer, an urgent knock at the door heralded the arrival of an excited Maurice Lindsay.

'Have you signed him?' Maurice urgently enquired.

'Yes, there's his Rugby League registration form,' I replied, as I offered it to the harassed Wigan director.

Silence.

'Bloody hell! That puts the pressure on me now, Ray. What am I going to do? We'll have to come up with something special now. Can you lend me some registration forms? I've forgotton to bring any with me.'

Flushed with success, I handed a couple to Maurice and, having chatted together regarding a few possible Wigan signings, he left to pursue his task. I'll never forget the look on his face when he returned half an hour later, not knowing whether to laugh or cry, as he shrieked, 'Geoff Sutcliffe's signature's at the bottom of the forms. If any players signed these they would be signing for Saints!' The St Helens secretary's signature was indeed at the bottom of the forms, an oversight on both our parts. A moment of light relief on a tense occasion, but few Wigan supporters realise how close Maurice Lindsay had been to signing John Ferguson for St Helens. He eventually captured another Central Park favourite, Brett Kenny, and Joe Warham and Harry Jepson returned home with a fistful of Australians, the most famous being Eric Grothe, the Kangaroos' flying winger. The influx of Australian players and eventually of New Zealanders had begun in earnest.

Unwittingly I had found myself in the vanguard of a movement which was to change the face of British Rugby League. In fact, the influx of Australians reached a ridiculous peak of no less than eighty-two players in the 1985–86 season, when clubs were swayed by any Australian accent, regardless of playing ability, and imports simply had to be restricted. I sympathised with the objections made by the RL Professional Players Association, whose lobbying finally reduced the maximum intake allowed to three overseas players a team by the 1987–88 season. None the less, with clubs like Hull, who added Peter Sterling to their register, Warrington with Les Boyd, Brian Johnson and Bob Jackson, and Hull KR who made early use of Gavin Miller and John Dorahy, there is no doubt that the influx did much to rekindle enthusiasm for the game.

As happened after the signing of George Smith and Lance Todd by Oldham and Wigan in 1908 after the first pioneering tour of this country by New Zealand, the League code was given a similar attendance boost, especially at the clubs whose adventurous overseas policy attracted the star players. The impact of Mal Meninga at St Helens, apart from bringing back cup success to the club, brought an average increase of 2500 spectators a game as well as increasing the crowds at numerous away matches. In two seasons Wigan's gates rose by 5000 a match while at Halifax, surely the success story of overseas adventure, the club was rescued from extinction. When the Yorkshire club's entrepreneurial president, David Brook, embarked on his sensational signing of eight Australian players in the summer of 1984 he came in for much public criticism, even ridicule. And yet, under the guidance of their former Kangaroo Test star, Chris Anderson, Halifax won the first division championship and restored the Challenge Cup to their trophy cabinet. In three seasons from 1984 Halifax moved from an average home gate of barely 1000 to attracting over 30,000 followers on their two Wembley trips in 1987 and 1988. And it is not without significance that in their first season after the return of the charismatic Anderson to Australia, Halifax once again found themselves back in the second division.

Such players have done much more than merely excite the crowds. They have helped to bring about a revolutionary change in attitude and approach to the sport which has benefited Rugby League's image in all sorts of ways. The Australian League player, accustomed to strict disciplines on and off the field in the intensely competitive Sydney competition, has brought those disciplines to the British game, on the field and in training. As well as helping to introduce better, more varied, and more demanding training schedules they have done so much to help change the attitude of the British players alongside them. Moreover, our players, especially the youngsters, are now much more professional in their commitment to the game and have helped to give it an athleticism which few team sports can match. The young are attracted to this new image which the Australians and, to a slightly lesser extent, the Kiwis have helped to cultivate.

Critics of the recent invasion of overseas players have gloomily prophesied, as a consequence, a decline in young home-grown British talent. They argue that British youngsters are unable to develop because of the overseas stars holding down their place in the team. The history of international rugby, surely the true barometer of the health of any sport, does not support such a view, nor do present trends in the game. During the immediate post-war period when Pat Devery, Johnny Hunter, Arthur Clues, Brian Nordgren, Cec Mountford and others trekked from Australia and New Zealand to find fame and fortune with British clubs, Britain experienced her greatest successes in Test rugby. Between 1946–62 Britain won seven out of nine Test series played against Australia. Since the introduction of the ban on overseas signings in 1977 Britain won only two Anglo-Australian Tests out of eighteen. As in the earlier period, I believe the influx from abroad has helped the development of our youngsters.

Players such as Garry Schofield and Lee Crooks as youngsters learned much by playing alongside Hull's star Australian and New Zealand imports. At Wigan, Shaun Edwards learned the art of stand-off play by observing from full-back, where he then played, the ploys of Brett Kenny in Edwards's now customary stand-off position. The effect of a season in the same pack as the Test prop, Les Boyd, can be seen in the growing maturity of Warrington's young tearaway forward Mike Gregory. The old maxim is true, that only by playing alongside the best will you become the best. Talented youngsters are encouraged by their better known team-mates and are given the impetus and incentives to succeed. And in 'incentives' is to be found another clue to the influence of the star imported players.

The vast sums of money now available to the leading players from abroad, some being offered contracts as high as £40,000 per season, have stiffened the resolve of our own players to earn the same with all-the-year-round rugby. Joe Lydon, Mike Gregory, Garry Schofield and Andy Gregory, by improving their skills and by raising their fitness levels, are now in demand by Australian clubs. Ellery Hanley and Martin Offiah have been paid a reputed £3000 a match in Australia. The full-time, all-the-year-round professional Rugby League player is now a reality and many of our youngsters are setting their sights on achieving similar goals, to the betterment of themselves and the game.

Talented players in France, where Rugby League standards have slipped alarmingly in recent years, are also looking to Australia as a nursing ground for their maturing abilities. International players, such as Jacques Moliner, Gilles Dumas, and Frédéric Bourrel, were encouraged to play in Australia in the summer of 1987 by the former French national coach, Tas Baitieri, in an effort to improve their standards; France's greatly improved showing in the two Tests against Great Britain in the 1988–89 season, and the improved health of the game generally in France, suggest that that experience may now be paying dividends both in team skills and disciplines.

Meanwhile, as the fortunes of Rugby League declined in the 1970s, that decade belonged most emphatically to Rugby Union. The feats of the British Lions, especially the exciting back play of Barry John, Phil Bennett, Gareth Edwards, Mike Gibson and others, raised the Union code to unparalleled peaks of quality. Now the 1980s have been captured by Rugby League, with the exhilarating try-scoring of Garry Schofield, the cheeky dynamism of Andy Gregory, the power and exciting running of Ellery Hanley, and the brilliant individualism of Martin Offiah. Many of its major matches, when shown nationally on BBC television, have generated tremendous enthusiasm. Indeed, such a knowledgeable rugby man as the great Cliff Morgan was moved to describe the 1985 Challenge Cup final between Wigan and Hull as 'the greatest game of rugby I have ever seen.'

In contrast, the often sterile and static play served up in recent Five Nations internationals, save for occasional flashes of inspired play from a Chris Oti or a Jonathan Davies before his conversion to League with Widnes, provides a pretty boring spectacle. The present standards of the Union code in the British Isles can often mislead when viewed in domestic isolation. However, there can be no mistaking our fallen standards after the disastrous Test match performances of England and Wales in Australia and New Zealand in the summer of 1988. England maintained their dismal record of never winning a Test match in Australia; and the second Test victory there for Australia by 28–8 was the biggest win in the whole series of matches. Wales's two catastrophic defeats, in which they conceded an amazing 18 tries to the All Blacks, represent the biggest margins of defeat ever recorded between two International Board countries. And Wales and Ireland's experiences against Romania and Italy left much to be desired. It was surely the turn of Rugby Union during the 1988–89 season in Britain to learn, like the League code, from the methods, attitudes, and players of the southern hemisphere. A continuing failure by Rugby Union to heed the lessons of the 1980s will simply consign the Five Nations tournament forever to the lower divisions of Rugby Union competitions. And the dramatic irony remains that, if Rugby Union in Britain is to compete with those nations in the premier division, then it must be prepared to spurn many of the old amateur attitudes which the leading nations have already done.

2

Union Problems

The long awaited Rugby Union World Cup in the summer of 1987 put the game, especially in the British Isles, under intense scrutiny, and those who watched all the matches which involved the four home unions must have despaired at what they saw. The results, despite Australia's defeat by Wales in a third place play-off, highlighted the wide gulf in standards between the major unions of New Zealand, France, and Australia and those at home. The dismissal of Scotland and Ireland at the first real hurdle, conceding over 66 points between them to New Zealand and Australia, was bad enough, but the low point for Rugby Union in the 1980s must surely have been Wales's 16–13 defeat of a ponderous, sterile England in a game described by Bob Templeton, the former Australian coach, as 'A disgrace! The All Blacks could play both of them at the same time and have both for breakfast'. And they duly did, defeating Wales to the tune of 49–6 and inflicting further humiliation on them during their summer tour of 1988 by registering a total of 106 points to 12 in two traumatic Tests. The England v. Wales match, coupled with the corresponding game at the Arms Park barely six months before, showed the depths to which domestic international standards have sunk in the 1980s. The free running of the England team in the home international against Ireland in the winter of 1988 when the wings,

Chris Oti and Rory Underwood, registered 5 tries must not be allowed to exaggerate the quality of the home championship and its players. My memories of Barry John and Mike Gibson toying with the All Black opposition, and the skills of Fran Cotton, Mervyn Davies, and Bill Beaumont making the South African forwards look ponderous, live still. But they are Rugby Union memories of the past, the lessons of the 1960s and 1970s having been forgotten in a headlong rush to mediocrity.

One cold Saturday afternoon in 1986, seeking refuge in my armchair from the frozen wastes outside and, for a change, watching BBC's *Grandstand* programme, rather than speaking to others from it, I was intrigued by the two Union internationals which were being featured. Within minutes of each other my two commentator colleagues, Bill McLaren and Nigel Starmer-Smith, were rightly focussing their attentions on the Scotland full-back, Gavin Hastings, and the England stand-off, Rob Andrew. And the object of their attentions? Both commentators were alerting their audiences to the fact that both, unknown to each other, were within sight of breaking the world record for the number of goals scored in an international Rugby Union match. Two players, on the same day, at venues only 400 miles apart, were being given the opportunity to enter the goal-kicking record books.

Here lies the problem with the Union code in the 1980s. The selectors, coaches, and players have forgotten that the prime purpose of the game is to score tries, the more the better for the enjoyment of both player and spectator. Bill McLaren, while commentating in one of the World Cup matches, also correctly said that the supposed founder, ultimately of both rugby codes, William Webb Ellis, 'picked up the ball, ran with it, and created the distinctive feature of Rugby Union.' As a description of the efforts of Fiji, Tonga, Australia and Japan this was a fitting comment, but today one might conclude that the distinctive features of Rugby Union in the British Isles is more of 'kicking the ball, catching it, and all falling in a heap around it'!

Throughout its history Union has rarely had to depart from being almost exclusively 'a players' game'. Most law changes have laudably been designed with the players foremost in mind but, as Rugby League learned very quickly, a game often has to change its laws and its approach if it is to attract and entertain sufficiently large numbers of spectators. When Rugby League broke away from the Union code in 1895, changes were necessary to generate the funds required to sustain the 'broken time' payments then being paid and, later, to allow for part-time professionalism. The amateurism of Rugby Union in the first 100 years of its existence has meant that the code's international law-makers have seen less need to adapt and change with the regularity of the League code. Thanks to the lack of any real professional or financial demands, until recently, on the Union game at club level in Britain, the need for law revision as a means of entertaining a paying, or more important today, a television viewing public, has been less demanding than on Rugby League's administrators.

By the end of the 1970s when British Rugby Union, thanks to an enlightened approach to coaching by such as Carwyn James and Syd Millar, was riding the crest of a wave, the law changes made immediately preceding or during those successful years were all taken from Rugby League. We saw the introduction of a new 'knock-on' law whereby the ball had to be knocked to the ground instead of being merely fumbled, a law which helped free-flowing back movements. More running with the ball was encouraged by the introduction of the differential tap penalty for certain offences, and even more enterprising play and creative running was intended with the introduction of the kicking dispensation law. A player under this law needed to bounce the ball in the field of play whenever he kicked the ball outside his 25-metre line instead of, as before, being able to kick directly into touch inside this area. The raising of the points value for a try from 3 points to 4 created a vital extra 1-point difference from the penalty goal, as was the case at the time in Rugby League, though League, quite rightly, have now increased that differential to 2 points. A League penalty goal now counts only 2 points as opposed to a try's 4. All such laws, taken from the League's law book, were designed to increase the flow of play, make for a more open game and encourage players to consider try scoring as the object of the game. And it worked for a time.

In the past decade the main preoccupation of the Union code's law-makers has been towards the safety of the players, especially in the scrummage and ruck areas where the incidence of broken necks and spinal injuries was proving counter-effective to the ideals of the sport. Thankfully much has been achieved in this area but most recent law changes have been mere tinkerings with those already applying and few opportunities have been created for the provision of more open rugby and for more exciting running from both forwards and backs. One change which should have added a new dimension to the game as a running spectacle was the introduction of the law allowing a player to pass the ball out of the tackle, immediately the tackled player made impact with the ground. But, as the international referee, Fred Howard, who took the third-place World Cup match between Australia and Wales, sadly declares, 'At almost every coaching session which I attend, the passing of the ball out of the tackle is rarely considered. All the coaches ever want to do is have their tackled player place the ball on the ground for the formation of a ruck situation'. England's 1988 tour manager, Geoff Cooke, looking for a sharp improvement in passing after the Queensland game, was widely reported in the press as saying, 'we have got to pass the ball before the tackle or take the tackle and hold on. The one thing we mustn't do is to pass while being tackled.' Enough said!

Rugby Union in Britain, at both international and club level (Bath, Leicester, Harlequins and certain Welsh clubs, such as Neath and Llanelli, being notable exceptions), has become the victim of the static nature of its laws, held in a technical strait-jacket and overburdened with a coaching philosophy which applies itself essentially to the static situations of the game. Such an approach has proved totally unsuccessful both in ensuring quality rugby on the field and sustained entertainment for those on the terraces. The law changes in Union, in contrast to those in League over the past decade, have been essentially cosmetic. Indeed, a drastic shake-up was suggested when Phil Horrocks-Taylor, the ex-England and Yorkshire Union stand-off, asserted in a newspaper article a couple of seasons ago the ultimate heresy so far as Rugby Union is concerned. He advocated the abolition of the two flank forwards and thereby the reduction of the number of players in a Union team from fifteen to thirteen. His idea, primarily to ensure more open running play, of removing 'the bully boy flankers who destroy the ambitious runners' was a dramatic intervention and one hardly likely to find favour with the International Board.

With players, at both Union and League, now attaining far superior fitness levels than their predecessors, an extra four players can have a cluttering effect on a game but, despite the lack of far-reaching Union law changes, the problem fundamentally is one of the attitude to coaching in certain quarters. That attitude, coupled with the blind acceptance by the governing bodies and the paying public's apathy towards the end product, usually results in an emphasis on avoiding defeat, by turning what should be a spectacle into an unedifying mess of mauls, rucks, line-outs, and scrums. And in these four areas of play lies the problem in the British Isles.

Almost ten years ago in *My Kind of Rugby* I wrote, 'Union has taken the best from League and has retained its basic strength, that of the wide gulf between forwards and backs. Though the rucks and mauls might seem an untidy mess to the casual spectator, with the line-outs all shoving and barging, they nevertheless have the function of bringing forwards together, taking them out of the game, and allowing space for the backs to run'. As I see the problem now, a decade later, these four aspects of Union play have been considered by many coaches to be the sum of the game itself. Their whole coaching strategy and effort revolve round these four set-piece events. The gulf between forwards and backs which I long considered to be a noteworthy feature of the Union code has now grown so wide that the backs often are hardly considered to be on the same pitch. The juggernaut sets of eight forwards test out each others' strength, often for the full eighty minutes, to the frustration of those who wish to see open rugby. It does nothing for the game and could lead to a serious decline in interest in Rugby Union. Hopefully England's fine performance against Australia in November 1988, enlightened coaching at Bath and Harlequins, for example, and the nurturing of youth rugby at Wasps and elsewhere could point the way forward.

There is no doubt that Rugby Union will have to learn to attract paying spectators and the wider television audience by bold and imaginative play at club level. Though internationals, club and county finals and other major matches can now fill Twickenham, the Arms Park and Murrayfield to overflowing, and attract valuable sponsorship money, the majority of club games are not well supported compared with the crowds that flock to see Widnes, Wigan and other principal RL clubs in the first division. Moreover, though it is good to see the leading Rugby Union clubs attracting valuable sponsorship, it is unlikely that they will ever be able to match the £250,000 that NORWEB put behind Wigan in the 1988–89 season.

We have reached a time when the television market will prove extremely competitive for all spectator sports, with a great deal of pressure coming from Rugby League, and the Union game cannot afford to become a backwater.

In Britain there seems to be a real (and totally mistaken) obsession with the role of the eight forwards. In the Five Nations championship of 1988–89 England averaged only one try per match, with just one from their supposedly exciting backs. Some excitement: some entertainment! In my international Rugby Union playing days I can rarely remember practising more than half-a-dozen scrums at any one session, and then the major reason for the practices was to enable the backs to rehearse their moves behind the scrum. There were no scrummage machines, there were no monstrous mechanical contraptions to practise rucking or mauling. And yet their absence seemed rarely to detract from the abilities of such props as Ron Jacobs (Northampton and England), Syd Millar (Ballymena and Ireland) and Hugh McLeod (Hawick and Scotland). Nowadays we have Rugby Union teams practising seventy or eighty scrums per training session with units of eight packing against metallic contraptions for the length of the field. Props appear from the inner sanctum of the clubhouse or the weight-training room, like some giant, squat, Sumo wrestlers with little athletic ability. On the field of play they pound from scrum to scrum, ruck to ruck, displaying few footballing skills save rarefied specialised techniques at the set pieces of play. Giants of 6 foot 7 inches, who leap and bound with abandon at the line-outs, emerge from this area like lurching, stiff, modern-day Frankensteins, bolts through their elbows, and shuffling round the field like floundering whales, many praying that the ball will never actually engage their hands in open play, such are the limitations of their athletic prowess.

In the back row we have again sacrificed the rugby skills of such as Tony Neary and Roger Uttley of England, or John Taylor of Wales, for even, at times, bigger unco-ordinated giants at the rear of the scrum than in the second row. Oh, for a British back row with the speed, athleticism, footballing skills and brain of the All Black trio of Wayne Shelford, Michael Jones, and Alan Whetton. The sole tactic of our no. 8 seems to be to hold the ball for as long as he can at the base of the scrum, allowing all the opposition defence in the backs to lie up flat and destroy any possible attacking chance. Once this has been achieved he will invariably try to pick up the ball and fall ingloriously in the hands of the opposing back row. The result being yet another scrum, ruck or maul.

Geoff Cooke, the England team manager, appears to share my concern, placing the blame for England players' obsession with set-piece play fair and square on the attitude of the clubs. In Cooke's official report following the 1988–89 season he had this to say:

> The most disappointing feature has been the reluctance or inability of players to fully embrace a 'total rugby' concept, which is, I believe, largely a reflection of what is happening in our clubs every Saturday. Far too much of our rugby is based on a safety-first approach, with an obsession for the set pieces and kicking as the main tactical planks. Few clubs appear to be working for the development of individual players and equally few producing any

> back play of note. Although the league programme has sharpened the competitive edge of our players and is developing greater mental toughness under pressure, we must be aware of the potential dangers of the fear of failure, which still seems to be an inhibiting factor at international level.

In contrast to the players of the southern hemisphere, France, South Africa and possibly Argentina, the British players, especially the forwards, are hardly finely tuned athletes, able to run, pass, catch and tackle. Most of the individual forwards are selected to perform a specific single function – to prop at tight head, jump at no. 3 in a line-out, or win ball at the back of the line-out. Few are selected for their athletic prowess in a game where speed of movement and speed of thought are, more than ever, paramount to success.

The British game continually parades players who have specialist qualities to win a team a ball against the head but who have no idea what to do with it when that ball has been won. New Zealand's play against Wales in the summer of 1988 highlighted the modern need for handling skills, power and pace in the forwards and for simplicity of approach and basic support play from their backs. Australia revealed forwards like David Carter, Jeff Miller and Steve Cutler, who can handle and pass the ball, and backs like Michael Lynagh and David Campese, who prefer to run rather than kick the ball. As one Australian critic, Greg Crowden, observed after England's lacklustre performance against New South Wales – 'They are still not free of their old defensive, conservative, boring habits, let the forwards fight it out, give the inside backs a sniff of leather . . . but for God's sake don't let them run with it. After all, the ball is there to be booted'.

Many of our Rugby Union coaches in Britain have

created a monster out of the eight front men who are devouring the game. The *cognoscenti* can appreciate the techniques used in a set-piece ploy, can applaud a feat of strength, but when performed *ad infinitum* and often apparently for their own sake without constructive relevance to the flow of the match, such actions are simply boring. The casual television viewer and the paying spectator demand more and, though I am myself an ex-forward and appreciative of the expertise involved, I ask for more than pushover tries which is all I seem to see whenever I watch our most successful Union teams. All sports are in a continuous state of development but British forward play, as it moves round like ancient Roman battle squares, solid and trusty, surely became an anachronism five years ago in the face of our competitors from overseas.

And what thought is being applied to back play and the cultivation of those priceless runners and handlers? Again I see little encouragement. Whenever the ball is finally released from the set-piece there is invariably a player selected in the stand-off position to kick as far upfield and as high as possible. Yet another Roman battle square forms as the end result of such aimless kicks. Creative centre play, such as we used to enjoy from Mike Gibson, and the subtleties of stand-offs like Phil Bennett and David Watkins are rarely approached these days in home internationals. John Rutherford of Scotland and Jonathan Davies of Wales have been the sole practitioners of the ancient art of running from the stand-off position. And if a player runs, where does he run to? Usually, like the eternal set move involving a winger, back into the pack on the receipt of the 'crash ball' to set up the 'second phase attack'. Rugby Union in Britain is now too rigid in its thinking, too stereotyped in its accepted views on positional requirements, and too blinkered in its refusal to accept the need to learn from overseas and from Rugby League.

The French have always retained their free running, often explosive, style of rugby save for the rare occasions when their coach Jacques Fouroux has demanded a strict forward game for a specific purpose, as in Nantes when France successfully defeated the All Blacks barely twelve months before the World Cup. Generally speaking, the game in France, both League and Union, is an expansive game with, in Union, forwards such as Rives in the early 1980s and Champ or Carminati today being expected to have the handling flair of a back – a style developed by those early League pioneers of 1934 and continued by such stalwarts as Jean-Pierre Clar, Max Chantal and the present-day loose forward Jacques Moliner. Both codes in France adopt from each other, the Union code not being averse to signing many top League players such as Jean-Marc Bourret despite the official anti-professionalism stance.

The New Zealanders play a simple game, relying on the athleticism, pace, strength, and handling skills of their pack to set up a mobile unit, capable of destroying any opposition and taking advantage of the many opportunities in loose play which this style of rugby affords. As with Rugby League's play-the-ball, when in possession from the set-pieces the ball is moved at speed with short crisp passes to centres who are close at hand, always, as in Rugby League, running parallel to the touchline.

Not for them is there any wide lateral passing behind the gain line as we see only too often in British Rugby Union. The result is that wings like John Kirwan, as with players in League, receive the ball well in midfield with room to use their pace and especially their strength. It seems to me more than a coincidence that whenever the All Blacks or the Kiwis play a Test match, the other code's team is usually to be found sitting in the grandstand or even visiting each other at training. Brian Lochore, the former All Blacks coach, and Graham Lowe, the former

Kiwi coach, have met and discussed each other's tactics many times. What a furore there was in Britain when Tom Hudson, the Bath fitness director, visited Hull Kingston Rovers, worked alongside their coach Roger Millward, and saw what coaching or playing techniques he could transplant to Bath.

Though Australia, by their accepted high standards, failed in the World Cup they have been one of the outstanding sides of the 1980s, illustrating how the game should be played. Their former exuberant coach, Alan Jones, may have remained too loyal to a number of his players for the World Cup, and a couple of his players may have reached their peak on the Wallabies' Grand Slam tour of the British Isles in 1985–86, but their performance highlighted the athleticism needed of all players and the pleasures for spectators of watching total rugby. Prior to that successful tour of Britain, Alan Jones studied Rugby League training methods in Sydney, chatted to top coaches and observed the national League team's style of play. He has even commentated on top League matches in Sydney. Much of the knowledge gained there was put to good use at home and abroad with the Wallabies on tour. Simon Poidevin, Australia's most capped player and the type of wing forward I have been urging, when interviewed in *Rugby League Week* magazine, hinted at his Union side's heavy reliance on the League code's fitness manuals: 'In Union we have taken note of the fitness methods of those recent Kangaroo teams as a feature of their successes. It is something we have adopted and we have leapt ahead'. He pays tribute to the League forwards' art of slipping the ball in the tackle and the close support work needed – the very slipping of the ball that the Wallaby forwards were able to indulge in during the British winter of 1986. And, above all, he pays respect to the far superior League defensive systems when he explains how, in that most defensively vulnerable of games, Sevens, he and his side learned from elsewhere. As Poidevin honestly remarks, 'Before the International Sevens final in Sydney against New Zealand I said to the blokes we are going out to play Rugby League defence, man to man. It worked'.

If, in future, the Union code in Britain is to promote itself as a healthy sport for youngsters, and it most certainly is that, then coaches must encourage the many gifted boys within its ranks to believe that athletic prowess will be rewarded and provide all with access to handling and running opportunities. The new league structures in English Rugby Union should begin to provide the mental and physical toughness, the necessary pressure rugby, and the vital competitive edge for modern players to thrive at international level. Here again much will depend upon the attitude of the individual players and the coach and ultimately, I think, upon the RFU's attitude to their biggest problem of the next decade, their approach to semi-professional Rugby Union in Britain, already a feature elsewhere in the world. All action, fifteen-man-handling Rugby Union can be achieved by good positive coaching.

In recent seasons the performances of Bath, Leicester and Harlequins in England have shown the rewards of encouraging flair. But, in South Africa, New Zealand, France and, to a lesser extent, in Australia something extra is added. It is patently obvious that the energies of players can be fuelled by lucrative financial inducements, direct or indirect, which can be made available. Here lies the RFU's problem for, to achieve the performance required and to meet the demands of modern international rugby, many players will be forced to achieve a level of commitment to the sport that calls in question its basic amateur principles. Nigel Starmer-Smith, the editor of the magazine *Rugby World*, admirably summed up the dilemma facing Rugby Union in this country when he posed a few questions in one of his editorials:

> Is such an approach acceptable in a game that espouses pure amateurism? Are the rugby authorities prepared to allow the preparation of an élite squad as a special case at the top of a game in which, for the overwhelming majority, it will happily remain a pleasant relaxation and leisure pursuit, combining some physical exercise with a lot of fun?

The newly formed league structures have and will no doubt continue to encourage greater attendances at club matches but as the code struggles to steer clear of, or to accept, a limited form of professionalism, it must now entertain those paying spectators as much as those playing the game. A professional sport like Rugby League, in its upper strata, is at the mercy of the whims of spectators. Its laws must develop with their entertainment uppermost in mind. Rugby Union is now faced with the same predicament but its style of play in Britain, like League in the 1970s, needs dramatic overhaul. Rugby League's style of play has increased its media awareness, encouraged a healthy rise in attendances, and now stands poised to reap the rewards of a much changed but vibrant approach to the game from the majority of its coaches and lawmakers.

3

League's New Dawn

Most sports have evolved after gradual adjustment to the original laws, needing to keep in step with the developing styles of the players on the field and the differing attitudes of the spectators round the pitch. Such a game is Rugby League. In its formative years, before the First World War, its law changes, in contrast to Union, were quite dramatic. The abolition of the line-out, the reduction of players to thirteen a side, and the introduction of the play-the-ball were all in the law book by 1907. Yet in recent years we have seen two events, one a law change, which have made a fundamental difference to the game. These two events, following and enhancing the introduction of the four- and, later, six-tackle rules in 1966 and 1972, whereby a side in possession of the ball was limited to the number of tackles it could receive, have definitely changed the styles of both coaches and players and the attitudes of spectators more than at any time since 1907.

I confess to being one who at first did not welcome the introduction of the limited-tackle law and did not see it as a way of halting the static and sterile play of the 1960s and 1970s. I anticipated that much of the play under the new rule would be frenetic with players playing a form of instant rugby rather like the modern fad for fast-food products, all froth and little substance. In the 1970s the rugby played was, on reflection, a hybrid with many players failing to adjust to the requirements of the new laws. However, by the 1980s, and especially now as we peer ahead into the 1990s, there were and are few who had experienced play under the old unlimited-tackle law of the pre-1966 era and so knew no other form of the game. They recognise, as we did not, that it has speeded up the game for every player, whatever his position, and has made fitness demands undreamed of twenty years ago.

Though the introduction of the four- and ultimately the six-tackle laws has obviously contributed enormously to the present good health of Rugby League, few of us could have foreseen the extraordinary effect of the hand-over law, when it was introduced in 1983. Following a meeting of the International Board, ostensibly to remove the Anglo-Australian transfer ban, this tiny adjustment to the laws was included at the end of a package of minor technical adjustments. And with what effect! The new law required a player in possession of the ball, at the conclusion of the sixth tackle, to 'hand over' the ball to the opposition. His opponent could then retain the ball for a further six tackles before he in turn was obliged to carry out the same procedure. A player could of course kick the ball on any one of the six tackles if he so wished and this he frequently chose to do for tactical reasons. The immediate effect of this new law was to speed up the game even more and to help individuals to develop new skills and roles within the game. The handover law was the change vital to complement the six-tackle change of the previous decade. If the experimental laws in operation in the British season of 1988–89 are applied internationally, then I envisage an even faster game with the emphasis on even more attacking rugby. The experiment to allow only one marker at the play-the-ball, instead of two, has removed the defensive concentration around that area while the necessity for players to line up at least five metres back from the scrum has had the desired effect of giving speedy backs extra space in which to run and produce intricate moves.

All tours made by Australian Rugby League sides to British shores are colourful, often controversial, but never dull; all, since the first made by those early pioneers in 1908, have influenced the direction of the game in Britain. Yet the impact made by the 1982 Kangaroos and by the equally brilliant tourists of 1986 was stunning. Not only did they become the first Australian tour party to win all their matches in Britain and the first to win three Tests but, in winning all the fifteen matches they played, they amassed 97 tries with spectacular rugby. Brett Kenny, Wayne Pearce, Wally Lewis, Peter Sterling and Mal Meninga became household names and their success was built upon their incredible standards of fitness, the detail of team plans, and the excellence of each player's rugby skills. Much of their approach on and off the field had been learned from American Football, and their performances and style captivated the public, both League and Union. The 1982 tour stirred the imagination and enthusiasm of all within the game to such an extent that, when the handover law of 1983 was seen to complement the exciting approach of those tourists and that of their equally famous colleagues in 1986, we realised that virtually a new game – and a spectacular one at that – had been evolved.

After that 1982 tour the demands for Rugby Leage of the type played by the Australians was insatiable. In response, we saw the appointment of Phil Larder, a former schoolmaster and Whitehaven and Oldham player, as the first full-time national director of coaching. Phil Larder then appointed a network of regional coaches capable of arranging courses and clinics for both professionals and amateurs. With a system of grading and the award of certificates, over 500 coaches qualified in 1988 through courses run by the National Coaching Scheme, often in conjunction with local authorities in both the north and south. The professional side of the game played its part by encouraging coaches and players to play the type of Rugby League which the laws and spectactors now demand by insisting that all the coaches in all thirty-four clubs in the professional league be qualified under the Coaching Scheme.

Many old pros insisted that such practises were a fashionable fad and not for them. 'We've been successful in the north for seventy years so what can the Aussies teach us?' was a popular cry from many reluctant to join in the mass conversion to the new ideas. The proof however could not escape them and, confronted with the success of the Australians and New Zealand in the Test series of 1984 and the further damaging exploits of the Kangaroos in 1986, the 'old pros' have for the most part merely faded away. The meticulous coaching approach and intensive training routines of Mal Reilly and his assistant, Phil Larder, on Britain's 1988 tour of Australia and New Zealand also indicated the way forward when, despite a horrendous injury list, their Lions side finally defeated Australia in Test rugby for the first time since 1978. Already the performance of clubs like Wigan and Halifax in the 1980s and the quality of rugby in the National Amateur League illustrates the value of the new approach to coaching and playing.

That new approach to coaching, further encouraged during the 1988–89 British season by Australian coaches such as Brian Smith (at Hull) and Darryl Van de Velde (at Castleford) and by British coaches like Mal Reilly at Leeds, has nowhere shown better results than at Halifax where Chris Anderson, the former Kangaroo tourist, worked with such success between 1985–88. Their ideas have since been adopted and adapted to suit the British style of play by Phil Larder in his great coaching manual and coaching proficiency schemes. While never neglecting an emphasis on individual skills training, this new breed of coach has introduced a greater awareness of the importance of self-discipline, has shown the need for higher standards of personal fitness, and proved the value of working with weights for physical strength. From training twice a week, usually in the evenings in my playing days, the modern player has had to adjust to an almost daily routine of training or coaching, has had to pay careful attention to his diet, and above all has had to maintain a disciplined approach to his game both on and off the field.

How has the League game managed to survive this concentration on coaching? Why should Chalky White, the highly respected former coach of the Leicester Rugby Union club, famed for its open approach to the Union game, now one of the RFU's technical advisers in the south-west, journey north to watch RL Test rugby as an aid to his coaching the Union code? The answers – the greater opportunities for an individual to display his skills and athleticism – can be gleaned from his admiration for the League code when he spoke candidly to *Open Rugby* magazine in 1986:

> I think this 1986 Australian team are, in world terms, offering the best team performance anywhere in any sport at present. Here are thirteen guys, highly skilful, extremely well coached, with a basic understanding of the game that is on a level quite foreign to many of our players.
>
> When we tried to find out what the Australians of 1982 did, and we saw that after they had finished training every day, Wayne Pearce would go out and do some more training on his own – that sets the tone for the whole attitude to the game – you realise you are dealing with dedicated athletes.

One sound argument often advanced for the superiority of the Union code over League is that players of differing shapes, sizes, and inclinations can form a Union pack whereas, today, a League pack tends to require players of a similar physique, speed, and agility. There is no doubting that the Union code, with its emphasis on scrums, rucks, mauls, and line-outs, needs the long, the tall, the round, and the short in their packs of forwards. But, unlike in New Zealand, France, and Australia, whose packs retain those physical qualities yet adhere to the athleticism and skills of a League pack, in Britain their roles are too limited and stereotyped. In League the fitness now required to play the game at the highest level is such that fitness schedules for modern players are quite horrific compared with those of barely ten seasons ago. Weight training, an asset in both codes for developing a player's bulk, is needed in League to encourage speed, whether the player be a forward or a back. And for a back, such is the intensity of the tackles and the need for power running in short confined bursts, weight-training is also vital for acquiring upper body strength. Whether forwards or not, all players in League need to be athletes to compete in the modern game, all need to be able to display individual skills like handling, running, and passing at speed and under pressure. The forwards especially, admittedly lacking the specialist roles of Union, are now superb athletes. Gone are the days of the ale-pot bellies on British props.

Successful converts from Union like Peter Williams (Salford) and Alan Tait (Widnes) willingly testify to the greater demands placed upon them by League and acknowledge the superior levels of fitness needed to be successful in that code. When one notes that in a League match the average player, while performing various skills and making strong body contact, covers 7000 metres at varying speeds during the eighty minutes of play, we can realise the need for vastly superior fitness programmes for the professionals. And when we realise that in an average League club game the ball is in play for fifty minutes as opposed to twenty minutes in a Union club game, then the words of both Peter Williams and Alan Tait bear out the advances in fitness made by Rugby League. Peter Williams, the former Orrell and England Union stand-off, insists that, 'League is a more explosive game than Union. Every time you run, whether in attack or defence, it is done at top pace. In Union you are merely jogging along from one side of the field to the other for the bulk of the match'. And the ex-Kelso and Scotland Union centre, Alan Tait, is even more critical of the levels of fitness at club level in Union: 'In a two-hour training session at League you are running all the time or smashing into tackle shields. The emphasis is on sharp sprint work and plenty of sustained running. It is very demanding. In Union, the backs were always stopped at set-piece practices, waiting to move with the ball'.

However, I believe the main reason why increased coaching in League has not stifled individual flair, as I have seen it do all too frequently in Union, lies in the difference in the number of players on the field and in the number of unit skills in which they become involved. Thanks to a reduction to thirteen players a side, the League game has only two static situations where a number of players collect together, and they, unlike in Union, number only twelve or fewer players at the most. Union has the scrum, the line-out, the ruck or the maul to collect together up to sixteen players or more, all, because of the technical and often precise nature of the formations, potential danger points for further stoppages in play and a delay to open running. Though the four methods of bringing the ball back into play in Rugby Union are, as I have indicated previously, demanding and interesting in themselves, they can and do often prove an untidy mess and, because of the unusually high incidence of them in an average match, have become the dominant feature. Here lies the problem, for many coaches in Britain place all their thinking on the four set pieces to the detriment of all else; and the tragedy is that success at only a couple of those unit skills can win matches without recourse to other players or individual skills. Not so in League.

The incidence of scrums under the new Rugby League laws has dropped dramatically from forty or fifty a match thirty years ago to twelve to fifteen today. The use of the play-the-ball, though possibly slightly higher than the number of rucks and mauls in Union, only occupies three men at the most, is simple, requiring few techniques, and thus, though repetitive, creates little delay in bringing the ball back into play. That there are only two unit situations in Rugby League has, sadly, in the past, led to neglect in coaching the skills of scrummaging and the play-the-ball but, thankfully, under the new coaching schemes, these two areas are at last receiving their due share of attention. I was greatly interested to see the 1988 Great Britain touring party in Australia and New Zealand paying keen attention to play-the-balls, both in attack and in defence, and laying great stress on the need for discipline around them. Unlike in Union, however, no emphasis can, or should, be placed on coaching those two unit skills.

Hence, unlike in Union, and for the eventual benefit of the game as an entertaining spectacle, most of the emphasis in the League code, whether in attack or defence, is on individual skills, especially those of running and handling. Once team fitness has been attained and an overall plan of a team's play and strategy has been developed, the emphasis will lie on an individual's execution of all the skills of the game. Many practices in defence using tackle shields will be done in groups, and a team's defensive strategy will be designed, but it is the individual player's tackling abilities and his alertness to the tackle that is being developed. In attack, individual skills, such as passing, kicking, handling, and running, are developed and harnessed to a team move or ploy but, in League, because of the emphasis on individual skills, the flair can rarely be stifled or neglected by a coach. It didn't take long for Terry Holmes, the ex-British Lion and Wales Rugby Union captain, to realise these crucial differences when he signed for Bradford Northern. 'The ball is always kept alive,' he has said. 'The game isn't built round stoppages and set-pieces as in Rugby Union; it's about continuity and getting the attack moving all the time'.

In general there is now a greater appreciation of the need to open out play, to move the ball wider by more varied methods, and to eliminate the boring forward drives down the middle of the field. When a couple of tackles have been absorbed by the forwards for tactical purposes, the backs are now usually calling for the ball. And the ball, because of the handover law, now has greater movement between the two sides. Hence kicking, a lost art in Rugby League to the 1980s, has come very much into vogue again and now plays a considerable part in the tactical plans of Britain's best teams.

In the Ashes series between Great Britain and Australia in 1988 the tactical kicking of the RL Lions side probably played a more prominent part in their tactics than at any time since the days of Jim Sullivan and Jim Brough in the 1930s. That magnificent win by Great Britain in the third Test was due in no small part to the long punts to the Australian try-line by Paul Loughlin and the short diagonal touch-finding kicks by the scrum-half, Andy Gregory. Loughlin's kicks, often sixty yards in length, exerted pressure on the Kangaroos' full-back, Garry Jack, and kept the Australians penned close to their line, unable to launch potentially dangerous try-scoring movements. The pressure forced them into mistakes while Gregory's kicks broke up the continuity of play and never allowed them to settle, whether defensively or in attack.

We have seen the introduction of a greater variety of kicks than before, and sides, knowing that they will ultimately regain possession, are now not afraid to risk losing possession with a kick in order to gain a tactical or territorial advantage. Players, in panic when under pressure, still do make long aimless kicks upfield in order to gain yardage and move away from their own 22-metre area at the conclusion of their six tackles, but the better players are now regularly using many varieties of kick. There are now no better exponents of the grubber or chip kick than Shaun Edwards and Andy Gregory, the Wigan half-back pair, who use the ploy frequently to break up the tightest of defences and to stop opponents from encroaching into the tackle too quickly. Joe Lydon (Wigan) and Paul Loughlin (St Helens) have perfected the long kick to touch into a fine art, flighting the ball with such accuracy that it performs the required bounce infield mere yards from the touchline. The up-and-under or bomb, as it is known today, is proving another useful means of exerting pressure on a defence. I welcome the increase in kicking in the game for, because of the need in League always to bounce the ball in play before finding touch, the kick is always used constructively and not, as with many of the less adventurous Union sides, as an easy option to running.

Such an increase in kicking within the game has meant that British full-backs, and to a considerable extent the wingers, who tend to lie deep in defence on the fifth or sixth tackle, must be safer catchers of the ball than they once were. Moreover, such is the amount of kicking now done by a full-back that it is no wonder that amongst the most successful British full-backs are four ex-Rugby Union players – Alan Tait, George Fairbairn, Steve Hampson, and Phil Vievers. The full-back's role now requires a player with speed who can take advantage of the many loose balls rolling his way from the broken fields in front of him, by running at speed to link up in attacks or to initiate those attacks from deep in his own half. The greater incidence of broken play in the game, with the ball passing to and fro between the sides at regular intervals, has led to a changed emphasis in the threequarter line where the centres now have possibly greater opportunities than the wingers. Sadly, wing play has declined somewhat under the new laws and the new approach to the game. Gone are the Van Vollenhovens of my era and there seem to be few signs of their replacements. Joe Lydon, potentially Great Britain's most dangerous wing, is a converted full-back. Martin Offiah, the former Rosslyn Park Rugby Union player, now with Widnes, is one genuine winger of the old mould, who is blessed with sheer pace.

Many wings are forced to look inside for their opportunities and there are a number of ploys which involve wingers in midfield coming to the fore. One reason for the decline in dashing wing play in the 1980s has been the reduction in the number of scrums, presenting fewer opportunities for clear-cut moves behind the scrum while the covering forwards are otherwise engaged. Thankfully, the necessity for backs to line up 5 metres behind the scrum under the new laws of last season, does seem to be encouraging wing play again. The forwards today, as a six, are not contained in the middle of the pitch, absorbing endless numbers of tackles, and thus their energies and greater pace can be used in racing to cover the touchlines.

We have also seen the decline of the slow but creative centre who was played only for the service he could give his wing. Nowadays centres are invariably big men, such as Michael O'Connor, David Stephenson and Paul Loughlin, able to absorb the strong tackling of the opposition and break through, or players like Garry Schofield who support well in broken play and capture 30 or more tries a season. Sheer speed, too, as with the Kiwi duo of Mark Elia (formerly St Helens) and Dean Bell (Wigan), is vital for the half chance. The speed of such players is now possibly greater than many of our present-day wingers.

The sheer pace and unrelenting movement of a Rugby League team today means that there must be a control point, a dynamo, from which the planning stems and from which the intricate patterns of movement originate. Prior to the last decade the axis for such movement was usually to be found in a skilful prop forward or loose forward, often working in unison with an accompanying scrum-half. Not so today, for the whole emphasis has switched to the half-backs who, for varying reasons, are now the lynchpin of any successful outfit. Peter Sterling, Brett Kenny or Wally Lewis have dominated the world in that position for Australia. Andy Gregory and Shaun Edwards bid to do the same for Great Britain and the first priority of all clubs is to have two hardworking and constructive half-backs on their playing register. The stand-off still performs the roles he has been playing throughout the history of Rugby League. He is still expected to create play for his threequarter line, support any forward breaks, and work in harmony with his scrum-half partner. With the loose forward now being forced to remain in the scrum until the ball emerges, the no. 6 is expected to perform a greater share of the tackling than he once did; no longer can he be covered by a fast moving loose forward like Vince Karalius (St Helens and Widnes) or John Whiteley (Hull). His partner in crime, the scrum-half, has been forced to take on a much heavier workload than before and, at times, a much changed set of duties.

Though a scrum-half needs to be quick at the base of

the scrum, adept at making a break down the blindside, and nimble enough to pick up the ball leaving the scrum and transfer it in one movement, his involvement around the scrums has lessened. The restrictions placed on the loose forward for movement out of the scrum has meant a decline in the moves at the base of the scrum between a no. 7 and no. 13, but, away from the scrum, his involvement has increased. In previous eras a large powerful prop like Brian McTigue (Wigan) or Brian Edgar (Workington) would monopolise possession and, by short or long passes, set up moves in midfield and broken play. Now, that task is usually undertaken by a scrum-half and such practitioners as Mike Ford (Oldham), Bob Beardmore (Castleford) and Andy Gregory perform that role. They coordinate the movement of the forwards in midfield and launch the backs when necessary with switch passes or longer passes to the flanks. To watch one of the world's best, say, Peter Sterling in action is to watch a study in perpetual motion. And not only in attack, for the scrum-half is also now expected to play a full part in defence, often acting as the last line of resistance in a soccer-style 'sweeper' role, a style favoured by Neil Holding of St Helens, for example. Yes, the forwards were once labelled as the donkeys for all the work they performed but, as their roles have changed, the scrum-half has assumed that mantle.

I have indicated earlier the rigidity of the playing roles in Rugby Union, especially in the forwards, where such is the precise definition of the positional requirements that only certain players of a particular physique can now fulfil that role. Such was the case in Rugby League until the mid-1970s with the six playing positions in the pack being possibly more strictly defined than even in Rugby Union. As in Union today, most League clubs strove to obtain the required blend and if it was achieved then it could give sides like St Helens, Wigan, Widnes, and Wakefield Trinity the successes they achieved in the 1960s and early 1970s.

The first League pack I ever played in contained this ideal make-up, inevitable perhaps, since it had been assembled by one of the finest forwards of his day, Alan Prescott, who in 1961 was the St Helens coach. Abe Terry weighed 16½ stone, stood 6 feet tall and used his bulk to control the scrums from his open-side prop position. In open play he would distribute the ball in midfield and often act as the pivot for the rest of the pack. His colleague in the front row, of similar dimensions, was Cliff Watson, whose specific jobs, apart from strong scrummaging, entailed bringing the ball away from the St Helens defensive area with strong surging runs and performing fifty or sixty tackles a match.

Hanging between them, the international hooker, Bob Dagnall, was selected for his ability to hook the ball from forty or more scrums a match, and any activity in the loose was a bonus. In the second row were paired a runner, Dick Huddart, who proved a prolific try scorer for Saints and Great Britain, and myself, the grafter and tackler, who was expected to provide the donkey work along with Cliff Watson. Behind, at no. 13, operated the finest loose forward in the world at that time, Vince Karalius, whose role, apart from his destructive tackles, was as a creator of play with delicately timed passes to his colleagues in the pack or to his backs running in support. Most clubs aimed for such a pack: not so today.

Nowadays, the front five in League tend to be somewhat similar to each other in physique, speed and skill, though perhaps the two props are slightly more bulky than the second row. Hookers, such as Kevin Beardmore (Castleford) or Phil McKenzie (Widnes), are selected not only for their ball-winning potential but, with only an average of twelve to fifteen scrums a match now, for their ability in open play. Indeed, I have often seen McKenzie perform for Widnes more than adequately in the stand-off position. Today many club second rows tend to be lighter than were Huddart and myself in the old days, there now being a limited number of tackles to absorb or break. Great Britain's second rows on the 1988 Australasian tour, Andy Platt, Mike Gregory or Roy Powell, combined the two roles carried out by the second rows of my era, being expected to tackle, run, pass, and score as regularly as possible; this was as instructed by all the most recent coaching manuals. The loose forward, though often tending to run a little wider, now performs a role similar to his second rows and few indulge in much creative ball work. Harry Pinner (Bradford Northern) is possibly the sole survivor of the ancient order of constructive loose forwards.

New Zealand and Australian internationals, such as Hugh McGahan and Wayne Pearce, are powerful runners and cover tacklers, equally at home in the second row. Great Britain's no. 13, Ellery Hanley, is an ex-international middle back whose power running and support play from the loose forward position enabled him to score 63 tries in a season in 1986–87. The modern League game is thus producing an all-purpose forward who finds it easy to adjust to any position in the pack since the requirements, save for a few remaining individual technicalities at the scrum and play-the-ball, are the same. Bob Louw, the former South African Rugby Union captain and flank forward, who recently spent two seasons with Wigan, likened our modern game to 'a cross between Union Sevens and American Football'. As he indicated, 'in a Union match I would only carry the ball in my hands for more than a few yards on perhaps six occasions, but in the League game I am given every opportunity to run, pass, or dummy with the ball and to take part in first or second phase attacks.' In such a conclusion lies the evidence, becoming more and more apparent, that the two codes, on the field of play, are now further apart than ever.

Such has been the change in the playing roles in Rugby League, so great has been the constraint under which Union players, especially forwards, play their parts, that it is now more difficult than at any time for a Union player to be successful in the professional code. League scouts are more wary as they stalk their Union quarry, and the potential convert must possess the style of play or skills which would make the gamble of his signing worthwhile.

Legendary ex-Rugby Union names such as Jim Sullivan, David Watkins, Lewis Jones, Dave Valentine, and Gus Risman, highlight the League code's debt to Union. In my own playing days at St Helens, our Cup-winning pack of 1965–66 welcomed four ex-Union forwards in Cliff Watson, John Warlow, John Mantle, and myself; none of us took long to adapt to the demands of the other code. Many clubs nowadays prefer to buy a seasoned League international from overseas on short-term contracts, confident that the Kiwi or Kangaroo will provide the goods. Other clubs who have wanted to dip into the wealth of Union talent in South Africa, France, and New Zealand have found it difficult to tempt players who are already experienced professionals within their own Union code.

However, Mark Brooke-Cowden, the ex-All Black forward signed by Leeds, and Charlie McAlister, Oldham's centre from New Zealand Rugby Union, provide possible evidence that the type of all-action New Zealand Union player, to which I referred earlier, could be future targets for Rugby League. There is certainly big money available to tempt outstanding Union players like Jonathan Davies, who joined Widnes in January 1989 for a world-record fee of £200,000, and Jonathan Griffiths, who signed for St

Helens from Llanelli RU for a reported £150,000. Others such as David Bishop (Hull KR), Stuart Evans (St Helens), Gary Pearce (Hull), John Bentley (Leeds) and Martin Offiah and Alex Tait (Widnes) have also turned professional during recent seasons for substantial fees. There is certainly no shortage of Union players wanting to join the professional ranks; though conversions to the League code have dropped from around thirty to forty signings a season in the 1960s to around a dozen today, all senior clubs report a substantial number of trialists coming forward from Union ranks. Three highly promising young backs who have turned professional in the last eighteen months are Brimah Kebbie (from Broughton Park to Widnes), Mark Preston (from Fylde to Wigan) and David Tanner (from Fylde to St Helens).

Once, League trialists had to be persuaded to play their trial game in some remote corner of Britain under the pseudonym of A. N. Other or S. O. Else in order to avoid recognition. Not so today, as the postman delivers letters daily to such clubs as St Helens, Wigan and Leeds from Union players, some of international standing, requesting a trial anywhere at any time. Some have even been known to forward a video of their try-scoring feats!

When Jonathan Davies signed for Widnes in January 1989, he captured the attention of the media as no other convert has ever done. Over 120 press men were present at Naughton Park for his first game as a professional against Salford. Due entirely to the Union star's presence in Rugby League the 13-a-side code won a place in the national consciousness that it had never previously known. Certainly Davies possesses all the skills to merit such attention and the former Welsh captain is just now at the peak of his powers.

David Stephenson, the Leeds and Great Britain centre and formerly a Fylde Rugby Union player, observes the situation well. Now in his tenth season of Rugby League, Stephenson was helped in his early days at Salford by having ex-Union internationals like Maurice Richards, Keith Fielding, David Watkins, and Mike Coulman alongside him. He is adamant that any intending convert would find the change today to be a traumatic experience. 'When I signed from Fylde I found a vast difference in fitness levels, and the tackling was unbelievable. I could break one tackle but always there was another coming.' Once over the induction period he had few regrets for, as he says, 'I do enjoy the game and love the atmosphere of playing before 15,000 crowds every week at Wigan, St Helens or Leeds'. However as I have stressed, and as David Stephenson indicates, the gulf in standards is now so wide, and the difference in playing styles so obvious, that it is his opinion that potential RL recruits from Rugby Union will be fewer. Says Stephenson, 'It is harder than ever for a player to switch codes because the two games have changed so much. In the forwards I can only see a Union flank forward having the pace, tackling ability, and footballing skills to make the change successfully. In the backs it is much easier but I can see few Union players in Britain having the running opportunities to impress their skills on a League scout'.

I agree with David Stephenson, but would certainly qualify Alex Murphy's harsh comments in his controversial newspaper column when, after watching a recent England Rugby Union international performance, he concluded, 'The only bloke in that outfit who might make it in Rugby League is the sponge man, who looks quite sharp on the move and might even be able to pass the ball.' Enough said, Alex!

In both codes there are still skilful young players thrusting forward from the junior ranks, capable of reaching the top, who would be fine exponents of rugby skills in either code. The young League players are involved in a sport which at last is making positive headway and providing a proper vehicle for the display of their talents. In Union, on the other hand, young players are involved in a game of immense potential, in terms of numbers of clubs and players at all levels of achievement, but meandering along, unsure of the direction in which it is heading.

Many clubs in the south-west, for example, or in Cumbria, another stronghold of rugby, be they Bath, at the top, or Berry Hill or Aspatria in the junior leagues, are striving above all for success at the highest level, sometimes with limited resources. On the other hand, an old-fashioned club like Old Reigatians, in the heart of the Surrey stockbroker belt, is content to remain a club that puts good rugby on a par with the social comfort of its members – and who is to say that there is anything wrong in that! But whatever the direction in which the two codes are heading and whatever the ambitions of individual clubs within the Union code, the harm being done to rugby by the present chaos in school sport is considerable and must be put right.

4

Back to School

The state of disarray facing both codes of rugby in schools, brought about by the pace of educational change and industrial action by teachers in recent years, is all too apparent. Yet, despite current attacks on the teaching profession for their disinclination to take on voluntary activity with the same degree of enthusiasm as was once traditional, the decline of team games, especially rugby, lies beyond the responsibility of individual teachers.

In today's larger schools, many head teachers no longer place the same emphasis on, or accord the same status to, their games' teachers as the now defunct grammar schools once did and as is still the case in the independent schools. Hence today's young teacher is often ill advised to cultivate team sports with endless hours of voluntary extracurricular activity for, in an educational world obsessed with 'curricular development', 'integrated studies', and 'pastoral development', the young sports-minded teacher has few rungs available to him up the career ladder. But the biggest single factor in the demise of rugby at schools is, simply, finance.

When various educational or sporting bodies pillory schoolmasters for not organising a rugby, soccer, or cricket team there always appears to be an assumption that sums of money are available to underwrite a sport. Here lies the problem, for there is no provision made by any government body to fund team sports in school, nor has there ever been. Sport is always mysteriously left alone to finance itself. A couple of pounds a head on school fees in an independent school will pay for all team games, and the master-in-charge of rugby has only to apply to the bursar for help. There is no provision for such help in the state sector and the numbers of staff who are prepared to work endless hours outside school, raising money for the funding of teams, is diminishing. Nor do I see that the introduction of the school teacher's 'contractual hours' contract, by which he is expected to work a set number of hours a week, will increase the willingness of staff, in the state sector, to undertake more voluntary hours on behalf of rugby. It is thus to the credit of the governing bodies of both rugby codes that they have foreseen this problem, have sought, in various ways, to bring in outside help, and are making strenuous efforts to counteract a decline of interest in schools by adjusting to the changed emphasis in education.

In my visits over the past twenty years to the Rosslyn Park Rugby Union Sevens tournament, the largest schools Sevens event in Britain, I have seen the entrants from the state sector in the north decline from over twenty schools to two. During my long association with the Lancashire Schools Rugby Union I have seen Union decline in a large city like Liverpool to a point where not a single state school now plays the game on a regular fixture basis. The number of schools still playing in Lancashire and other counties is swelled by many who rarely play a fixture but whose affiliation to the English Schools RU gives staff ready access to senior international match tickets. The Scottish Rugby Union recently calculated that the code in Scotland is played by approximately 5000 boys between the ages of twelve to eighteen years as opposed to 15,000 a few years ago.

My own county schools' governing body, despite the millions of pounds coming into Rugby Union from sponsorship by national companies such as British Gas and Save and Prosper, has rarely received any financial help from central finds save an annual grant of approximately £2000 from the Lancashire senior body and the Middlesex Sevens memorial trust fund. Such a sum is dependent on the success of county Rugby Union, by virtue of gate receipts, at a time when clubs are downgrading county rugby. To their credit the RFU has asked clubs to appoint liaison officers to co-ordinate help for schools in their area but, apart from generous help with facilities for county matches from clubs like Waterloo, Ruskin Park, and Vale of Lune, or small amounts of sponsorship money from the St Helens / Liverpool club, as in my own school's case, there is little help forthcoming. The technical officers appointed by the RFU to help develop the game can have little effect, such are the vast distances they have to cover. The organisation of coaching courses and yet more coaching courses appears to be their sole justification, and yet the performance of our England national side over the years would indicate that their work is hardly cost effective.

The once great strength of the Union code within the state educational sector – the vast numbers of schools once playing Rugby Union the length and breadth of Britain – is now, ironically, one of its greatest weaknesses. It is well nigh impossible for the RFU, unless there is a drastic change in policy and income levels, to help fund individual schools. Nor can the clubs, themselves grappling with financial constraints, be too generous to schools within their area. As John Dewhurst, the long-serving secretary of the Lancashire Schools RFU, has said, 'The game has survived so far on small bodies of absolutely devoted people who approach things in an amateur way. But the game is going professional with a small p and that approach will not suffice much longer.' There is no doubt that schools Rugby Union, though not by design, has contracted to its original base of the independent schools who will be expected to bear the brunt of producing future internationals. In a changing social world I do not believe those schools will be capable of sustaining the growth needed to maintain the Rugby Union's dominance over Rugby League.

With Rugby League the code has traditionally experienced a narrow schools base in the three counties of Lancashire, Yorkshire, and Cumbria where the sport, in the Rugby League playing towns especially, has remained the focal point of the pupils' attentions. Here there are welcome signs that that base is to be strengthened and fostered to an extent not previously known while, ironically, moves are afoot to widen the impact of Rugby League in schools in Sussex, Surrey, Hertfordshire and the Isle of Man. Also, in Sheffield, the hard work of the Sheffield Eagles club manager, Gary Hetherington, aided by the city's education department, has seen the rise of a schools League tournament in this once virgin territory. This is a welcome trend within schools Rugby League, but a trend which is minute compared to the way in which Rugby Union has expanded in the past. The parochialism, once the weakness of England Schools Rugby League, might perhaps become its strength as it too seeks to regroup and strengthen its hold over pupils and willing staff who have experienced similar problems to their Union counterparts. Here the League code is in no better or worse state than the Union code but I am optimistic that its prospects at base are brighter. The League authorities are, both by accident and design, embarking on a path which I definitely believe to be for the future good of schoolboy Rugby League.

The 11–16 age group has shown a slight resurgence over

the past couple of seasons with the introduction of more cup competitions based on a wider entry and the continuance of the highly competitive tournaments built round town teams. Matches continue at international level with France on a regular basis, and many adventurous schools still embark on annual trips to play in France, Oldham schools trekking further afield to Australia in the summer of 1988. And yet the most significant development, and surely the hope for the long term future of youth rugby, is the formation of a network of local Rugby League development officers under the aegis of the British Amateur Rugby League Association and local authorities. Such appointments in Sheffield, the north-east, and the south-west of the country are vital for expansion and those in areas like Leeds, Wigan, and Rochdale are vital for the consolidation of the sport. Again, we see the League code, like its rival Rugby Union, whether by choice or accident, reverting to its original base – only, I believe, unlike Rugby Union, with a more optimistic future.

Leeds City council was first into the field with the appointment of Maurice Bamford, then the Great Britain coach, as their development officer. Under Maurice's brief to teach the basic skills of the game to school children, provide Rugby League entertainment at local sports centres, help create teams, and provide specialised coaching to any gifted individuals, the project was immediately a huge success. West Yorkshire metropolitan council soon weighed in with £150,000 for the purchase of new headquarters for the amateur authorities in Huddersfield, while the Greater Manchester council financed a 'centre of excellence' in Leigh at a cost of £180,000. Here youngsters can take advantage of new pitches, a multi-gym, and floodlit training areas. Rochdale, too, have appointed their first development officer, significantly an ex-schoolmaster, to organise the setting up of junior leagues. Councils such as

Leeds, who have purchased Elland Road, the home of Leeds United soccer and Hunslet Rugby League club, and Bradford Council, where extensive work has been carried out on the Odsal stadium, are also ploughing many millions of pounds into Rugby League stadiums. The relationship between council and Rugby League is a fast developing one, and one which must help to rectify any weakening of League strength at schools level.

Rugby Union has also seen the need to cater for boys no longer taking part in regular rugby sessions in school by encouraging mini-rugby at clubs and urging those clubs to extend their team structures to cover youth sections. But this system is being operated, as John Dewhurst observed, on a professional basis 'with a small p'. The link between schools, amateur Rugby League, and the town councils is Professional 'with a large P'. Schools Rugby League will continue to thrive, nowhere more so than in the Under-11s age-group. The sight of those youngsters who annually play the curtain raiser to the Rugby League Challenge Cup is testimony to the skills learned at this tender age. The likes of Joe Lydon, the Wigan and Great Britain star, will continue to take their first steps into Rugby League's Hall of Fame on lush Wembley turf as an eleven-year-old. Rugby at other age levels may not remain the dominant feature of a school's team sports but, whether for the school, the town team, or the amateur club junior side, the alliance of schoolmaster and council officer will steer schoolboys in the direction of Rugby League.

The greatest satisfaction of my rugby life has sprung from my twenty-seven years involvement with schools rugby of both codes. Now it may sound like heresy to welcome the intrusion of outside bodies into what was once considered the teacher's preserve. But, sadly from the teacher's point of view, I believe that the future development of League and Union will slip away from the teacher's grasp and clubs will have to learn to provide rugby for youngsters.

This is already being successfully achieved at clubs like Bath, Leicester, Wasps (who have taken the trouble to explore the youth set-up at Agen in southern France and are determined to build youth sides of quality), Saracens, and doubtless others across the country. Indeed, any spectator fortunate enough to have watched a Wasps v. Leicester colts match one blowy afternoon in February 1989 would have been favourably impressed by the team skills on view. And Bath's nurturing of Jeremy Guscott through every age-level at the club, from mini-rugby to 1st XV, brought the player his first England cap and British Lions' representative honours in the summer of 1989.

A recent trend in education has been the promotion of 'community schools' into which vast sums of money have been poured for the laudable purpose of encouraging adults, living round the school, to participate in a wide range of activities and courses. 'Crochet for Beginners', 'How to Handle your Teenager', 'Yoga for Pensioners' are all courses which have been funded by local authorities to promote a community spirit. Yet alongside such schemes our councils fail to provide any funding for team sports at the very same schools. If our councillors took the slightest interest in school sport they would see what an asset a school's sports team can be for the surrounding community. They would realise the potential involvement in the school of parents, friends and old pupils, on behalf of the sports teams, without incurring huge sums of money. In Rugby League, areas such as mine in St Helens, Wigan and Wakefield or in Rugby Union districts like Bristol, Bath, or Aberavon there is to be found a comradeship, a spirit, and a fierce local pride which welds together a school and its neighbouring community. Nowhere has that been more apparent than in my own town of St Helens and at my own Cowley School.

Before any sport can be played at school many thousands of pounds have to be raised by voluntary means; in the case of Cowley School this is to finance not only our regular rugby fixtures but to offset the cost of the tours we have made to South America, Canada, Australia, Holland, France and Portugal. Raising approximately £300,000 over a twenty-year period may prove daunting for any young schoolmaster, but it can be done. Given a dash of boldness, a touch of ingenuity, and above all, good old fashioned 'cheek', any obstacle can be overcome.

Such levels of fund-raising must be approached as a military operation with pre-season strategy meetings and constant scrutiny of the financial markets. But, once our intrepid schoolmaster has embarked upon such a task, he is heading for a most exciting and humorous life-style. Sponsored events, discos, wine and cheese parties, treasure hunts and donkey derbies are the staple diet of all amateur fund-raisers, but to hit the financial jackpots the rugby master must seek out the unusual, the exotic and, best of all, the blatant confidence trick if he is to capture the public's imagination and reach the public's purse.

School galas can be quite sedate events with the local celebrity or headmaster presiding over the afternoon's affairs with a bemused smile, and patting the heads of his charges as they toil at the hoop-la stall or roll a penny. Nodding appreciatively, headmasters will transmit silent thanks in the general direction of the mothers who pour out endless cups of tea and offer cucumber sandwiches to an eager public. Many such fund-raising events can have a genteel socialising effect. Not so at Cowley School: in our attempts to rival Barnum and Bailey in the exotic, our patrons were tempted to take their life into their own hands or even risk the loss of a limb, all for a good rugby cause. Especially when an alligator came to town! What better fund-raising gimmick could be launched than to organise a giant raffle at a gala with the offer of an alligator as first prize? Surely the dream of every youngster is to keep one in his bath at home. Cowley intended to fulfil that dream for some unsuspecting child.

In conjunction with an ex-Union playing colleague of mine, Wally Ashcroft, who had just opened a pet shop in town and welcomed the publicity, we devised the idea of holding the raffle. A marquee was erected and a fishpond constructed in the school's quadrangle to display a huge collection of hamsters, goldfish, rabbits, gerbils and budgies. For the purchase of a winning ticket any youngster, accompanied by his parents, could take a voucher to Wally's shop and, once they had been carefully vetted as to their genuine intentions of looking after the prize pet, they were rewarded. But the alligator, the star prize, would be presented at the gala!

The publicity expected duly came in the form of an outcry from the RSPCA who queried the exotic reptile's safe keeping on the school site and the danger to the public. Long before its arrival, our headmaster, Walter Wright, was driven to despair by the attentions of a national daily newspaper which ran a scare story of a wild alligator seemingly kept in a school cupboard, and about to be carried home on the no. 6 bus under the arm of a young prize-winner. 'All good publicity,' as they say in the trade. Finally the day arrived, thousands flocked around the school grounds, and large queues formed outside a classroom which had been specially cordoned off and displayed a huge poster 'Danger – Wild Alligator Inside'. At precisely 1 p.m. a two-ton Hertz truck left Wally Ashcroft's shop and made its way slowly through the town centre until it arrived, to the consternation of the throng, alongside the classroom. The large truck doors were opened flush with the outer school wall and, hidden from view, a vast container carried in. Excitement mounted, the RSPCA inspector craned his neck, and the headmaster consulted his insurance documents. The first visitors into the darkened room groped their way towards a two-foot aquarium tank, placed on a table in the middle. Alongside lay a large magnifying glass through which to view the star prize – a two-inch stick alligator! 'We've been done. He's done us again!' were cries that rent the air when incredulous but smiling customers left the darkened room. True, but there were even bigger smiles on the faces of the rugby staff when we deposited the huge profits from the gala in the night safe of the Midland Bank.

To organise such events a rugby master needs to develop the talents of an impresario and scour the showbusiness newspapers for his crowd-pulling acts. Acts like the human mole whose job was to burrow under the school long jump sand pit, and emerge two hours later, when customers had placed flags, as in a treasure hunt, to mark his exit. Or I could recommend a fire-eater, so long as he didn't set fire to the stage curtains and singe the hair of the parents in the front row of the hall as he did at one of our functions, thanks to an overdose of petrol. Why not try the open-air circus which I billed in the local newspaper as the equal of Billy Smart's for spectacular acts? The circus duly arrived in a battered Austin A4 van, out of the back of which poured a man, his wife, a dog and a monkey. What more could I expect for a £50 booking?

Perhaps one of the most time-consuming, back-breaking, and hardly to be recommended fund-raisers is the collection of waste paper, a task we accomplished with over 100 tons to help finance our trip to South America. I can still picture the relief on my headmaster's face every Friday evening when the weekly six-ton load, hidden from the sight of any prying school safety officer, was taken to the waiting lorry by a class of willing helpers . . . well, *mostly* willing helpers. When given the choice of loading a lorry with waste paper or of continuing with the construction of Latin verbs for the last period on a Friday afternoon most fit, healthy boys chose the waste paper. Only one once remained reluctant.

'But, sir, my mam has just bought me a new blazer. It's my first day wearing it. If I help carry your paper, it'll get dirty,' was the cry of one small naive youngster who had no wish to exert himself. His new blue blazer with its shiny embossed badge was to be his defence. But there was no defence, save an occasional whimpering in reply to my suggestion to take his blazer off.

This he promptly did and, with his help, the six-ton pile of paper was loaded. The lorry driver paid his dues and headed through the school gates to the pulping machine. At the conclusion of our efforts I was left alone, mopping my brow, save for the attentions of the still whimpering youngster.

'Sir, sir, my coat, my coat,' he moaned.

'What's the matter, you can't have got it dirty. I told you to put it down somewhere,' I replied.

'I did, sir. I put it down on the back of that lorry. It's gone off in the waste paper.'

Not one of our most profitable days!

Nevertheless the tours for which the money was raised were extremely profitable to our community, especially in giving the lads a taste of international rugby, cementing that special bond between master and pupil and, above all, enabling us to continue our hilarious way throughout an incredible rugby world. Being one of the masters in charge of a first-ever trip by any school to South America in 1972, to play Rugby Union in Argentina and Uruguay, filled me with an intense pride but, once there, I doubted whether I would ever emerge from its Amazonian jungles, such were the hazards with which we had to cope. As if it wasn't enough to be told, on the eve of our departure from Buenos Aires, that the travel company had gone into liquidation, thus causing us to travel home on every conceivable aircraft bar a Wellington bomber, our experiences, on arrival in Montevideo, Uruguay, were to say the least, disconcerting.

Our party's misfortune, on embarking from the overnight ferry across the River Plate, was to arrive in Uruguay on the same morning of the assassination of one of the country's top naval commanders by the Tupamaros urban guerrillas. Panic ensued. Nerves began to fray when our coach was stopped within yards of the docks to allow troops, with machine-guns in hand, to search us most thoroughly. An odd comment from a staff colleague, Bill Dixon, caused a gun to be placed against his head. Nor did it help one's composure when another colleague, Derek Parr, and I found that the assassination had occurred close to where we were staying, the dried blood still staining the street. Under careful instructions from the master-in-charge of rugby at the British School, Montevideo, with whom we were staying, we were advised to beware of strangers and listen for gun fire. Nervously we both crept into bed that night only to be stirred minutes later by the sound, seemingly, of machine-gun fire. I met Derek under the bed. Silence. Furtively, slowly we manoeuvred to our feet. Only to find the metallic blind had risen accidentally to the top of the window frame. So much for the splutter of machine-gun fire! So much for the Tupamaros guerrillas.

My own security and that of the accompanying staff, Derek Parr and Dave Watson, was also uppermost in my mind one fateful morning during our trip to Canada during Easter 1976 when all three of us were 'confined to bed' for a short stretch. On arriving in the suburbs of Toronto late at night and being informed by our Canadian host that we could have the luxury of a lie-in in bed next morning while he went shopping for breakfast, we gratefully leapt into our makeshift camp beds on the lounge floor. He never told us about his pet. Imagine our surprise and fear when, upon waking, my attempt to remove the blankets was greeted by the loudest of growls and the baring of the most hideous set of teeth I have ever seen so early in the morning. A veritable hound of the Baskervilles sat guarding us from his perch on the chair between the beds. There was no escape. How we cursed the beer of the previous night but incontinence was to prove the lesser of two evils until hours later when his master returned home.

Perhaps one of the most satisfying moments of a hectic rugby life, when on tour in Australia in 1981, was not the delight at defeating the highly competitive Australian school teams in all thirteen matches played but of using my previous experience to overcome a tactical ploy presented to us. The hospitality afforded to our party by the Rockhampton Grammar School was exceptionally lavish with a large villa placed at our disposal at Ritamada, a peaceful deserted beach on the shores of north Queensland. Amid sun, surf, and palm trees and fortified with a regular supply of pineapples and steaks for our barbecues, we enjoyed an idyllic three days in which to prepare for our match. A time for swimming? A time for fishing or touch rugby on the beach? A time for developing that bronze tan? Certainly not!

As one who, being fair skinned and lacking a full covering of hair on top, had suffered from the tropical sun when touring with the Great Britain Rugby League World Cup team in 1968, I sensed the dangers and a possible trap. I immediately set about to fine any lad caught without a T-shirt, whether swimming or not, the sum of one Australian dollar. Countless groans rent the air as my flat cap appeared from behind rocks overlooking secluded caves in my search for the occasional bare torso. Chests were hastily covered up at the sight of my footprints in the sand. My lads, and the staff, feared for my mental health and felt that I had cracked under the glare of the midday sun, but I was to be rewarded when, in conversation with a parent of one of the opposition, a casual remark justified my fears.

'Did you have a good time at Ritamada? Have you had any sunburn?' he queried.

'No'.

'That's unusual,' he replied, with a disconcerted look on his face, 'The last touring party lost the whole of their front row with sunburnt backs. We won every scrum that day'. Our final result of Cowley School 29 Rockhampton GS 6 proved my mental faculties were still in good condition.

A rugby life is a difficult one for a present-day schoolmaster, its rewards are often not tangible, but anyone observing the tears in my eyes, and those of my players in the dressing-room at the successful conclusion to our Australian tour, would have no doubt over the emotional depth of those rewards. Sadly, however, I was to experience further tears a few years later with schoolboy rugby, only this time they were to come from experiences initially beyond my control.

A telephone call to my school staff-room at 10.30 a.m. on Tuesday, 29 November 1984 was to occupy my rugby thinking over the next six months, with dramatic conclusions for both the Rugby Football Union and myself. Ian Sinclair, a friend of many years standing and chairman of the Lancashire Schools committee, told me, much to his embarrassment, that I had been banned by the RFU from playing any active part on the schools committee because of my previous League connections. I was stunned to learn that after twenty-three years of work on behalf of Lancashire Schools I was to be ostracised under their law

3.9, Teacher Participation, which stated, 'A qualified teacher in full-time educational employment may be allowed to organise and coach the game within the sphere of education for which he is paid by a recognised education authority.' In other words, I could work on behalf of Cowley School but I was to be kept firmly locked inside my school gates. Work for the Lancashire Schools RU had come to an end.

The ban dramatically, stupidly and, I believe, much to the embarrassment of sincere people like Bob Weighill, the secretary of the RFU, opened up all the old unnecessary antagonism between the two codes of rugby. It was to prove a sad event at a time when those wounds, once wide and glaring, were healing by natural process. Furore raged in the press for weeks at the shame of my treatment. I received sackfuls of letters of support from all parts of the Union-playing world, and I even received an apology from Twickenham for being 'treated harshly and discourteously' by the Lancashire RFU in the manner in which my ban had been announced. But I still remained an outcast. All the outcry would have disappeared in time and I would merely have been left as the centre piece in one of the endless Union/League squabbles, which used to leave League regularly as the defeated party. It was not to be on this occasion for I determined to take up the cudgels, not so much on my own behalf, but on behalf of others and for the future of the teaching profession.

Though I had been selected as the victim, the implications for other schoolmasters in my position were far more serious since I would readily admit that I do not expect further promotion within education. Yet teachers, such as John Bevan, Clive Griffiths, Alan McInnes and John Knighton, to name but a few former League players who had been coaching Rugby Union at school, could have been restricted in their careers by being unable to take part in full extra-curricular activities. The new assessment of teachers and the accompanying pay structure to be introduced would cause difficulties where one PE teacher would be judged against another who had been allowed to take part in all outside activities. The latter's experience would further his career at the expense of the ex-Rugby League teacher. This was obviously a restraint of trade. And, as one who paid considerable taxes to a Sports Council which was part funding Rugby Union under the slogan of 'Sport for All', I was naturally aggrieved. Despite the cries of anguish from within and without the Rugby Union establishment, the governing body of the code had no intention, initially, of deviating from their active discrimination against me.

I was hurt but under no circumstances would I become yet another example of Union victimisation when, as Paul Fitzpatrick of the *Guardian* declared, 'French has probably done more to promote Rugby Union at grass roots than those who have banned him'. Armed with legal opinion, given gratis by an ex-rugby playing pupil, and briefed by Queen's Counsel, I determined to attend the next committee meeting on Tuesday, 15 January 1985. Like Don Quixote I picked up my lance, mounted my white charger, and set off with my trusty Sancho Panza (Ray Jones the Schools treasurer) from my home in St Helens and rode up the M6 to the Trafalgar Hotel, Samlesbury. The battle commenced but there was to be no tilting at windmills.

Drama ensued when, with a bevy of press men waiting in the hotel lounge, at 7.30 p.m. the chairman, Ian Sinclair, on advice from the Lancashire RFU, declared that the meeting would be unconstitutional if it was held in my presence. A daring decision but one which was to provoke instant reaction from the assembled schoolmasters. On a proposition from Shaun Higgins, of Lancaster Royal Grammar School, it was declared that the meeting continue with me present and, ultimately, in the absence of the chairman Ian Sinclair. He left. He had been placed in an invidious position as the one who had to fire the bullets on behalf of a group of faceless men but sadly for them it was to be the RFU who were shot.

My case was heard, considered, and accepted. And to the eternal credit of the schoolmasters they supported my stance unanimously. It was obvious that, when the committee reserved the right 'for any constitutionally elected teacher to sit on the schools committee regardless of any connection with Rugby League and without exception', eventually I would triumph. Despite the RFU's sudden new found enthusiasm, following the meeting, to seek a change in the law governing schoolmasters at the next International Board meeting four months later, the Lancashire governing body continued to press for my expulsion from the next meeting. I was especially amused at the vehemence of the hue and cry for my scalp when John Burgess, one of Lancashire's representatives on the RFU, was quoted as saying, 'I was astounded to discover it had been going on for almost twenty years. But it is clearly against the by-laws. The laws cannot be ignored as a matter of convenience'. My name, as a representative on that schools committee, had of course been placed annually before the senior Lancashire Rugby Union committee for those past twenty years.

It was only in deference to my good friend John Dewhurst, the schools committee secretary, who had been most understanding of my predicament, that I agreed to a postponement of the committee meeting until after the International Board's decision. The outcome of that fateful International Board meeting, held in Paris, was that my actions were completely vindicated and I was at last to receive a letter from the beleaguered, and I think somewhat relieved RFU secretary, Bob Weighill, pointing out that the law had been changed and that I and others in a similar position could now indulge fully in schools rugby at all levels. Ian Sinclair was now able to express his true feelings when he declared, 'We owe Ray a great deal and he would have been sorely missed'.

Thankfully this sad contest between myself and the Lancashire RU was over but I believe my victory over the Rugby Union's reactionary laws proved, in the words of Maurice Oldroyd, of the British Amateur Rugby League Association, to be 'a super catalyst in the controversial issue of a "free gangway" between the two codes at amateur level and one which we hope will bring matters to a head'. Within eighteen months that hoped-for 'free gangway', whereby amateur players of all ages are allowed to play both League and Union, was conceded by the RFU, admittedly not without a little pressure from myself along the way. The sheer idiocy of the Lancashire Rugby Union's attempts to ban me from my activities with the county's schools union was amply illustrated exactly two years later when, after the complete collapse of the three schools committees in the south-west, south-central, and south-east of the county, I was the only teacher still prepared to organise school trials for the 1988–89 Lancashire Schools Under-18 side.

It has taken ninety years for the RFU to appreciate that public attitudes have changed both inside and outside the body of Rugby Union. Social changes and more mature attitudes have led to a totally different view of the League code; its undoubted success in the 1980s has been recognised and will lead, I feel sure, to the consolidation and expansion of the sport in the 1990s.

5

Times are Changing

Though our present-day educational system may be experiencing problems in maintaining the conveyor belt of rugby talent – both League and Union – which flowed from the schools in the 1950s and 1960s, higher education may ultimately hold the key to further national and international expansion of Rugby League. The League's future image-makers, its new administrators, sponsors, and possibly its players, may already have been produced over the past ten years at various colleges of higher education. We may already now have, waiting in the wings, those very people to perform the services for the code that the similarly placed 'old boy' network did so effectively for Rugby Union. As we assess the possible path of Rugby League's development, we would do well to reflect on the history of Union development at both national and international levels. The explosion of the Union code all over the world, compared with League's limited international expansion, has been a salutary lesson for Rugby League's administrators but a lesson from which they have learned much. And, given sensible homework over the next couple of years, they might just regain the initiative lost over ninety years ago.

Criticism has been and still is rife within the League code over its management's supposed lack of direction and its past inability to expand significantly beyond its long held national and international boundaries. We have always been told that Rugby League did not possess the right image, and have frequently had marketing consultants foisted upon us to improve that image, often regardless of the financial implications for the sport.

Meanwhile, Rugby Union has been viewed through misty eyes by the *cognoscenti* of the League and regarded as the image to present to the outside world. I would take issue with the *cognoscenti* for I believe they steer clear of two aspects of the game which have, until the 1980s, blighted Rugby League. I accept that at times many within the sport have become obsessed with the old northern music-hall profile (not that I believe there is anything inherently wrong in that) and have assiduously cultivated an air of inverted snobbery in attitudes to the south. In its heyday in the 1940s and 1950s Rugby League missed its way for national expansion by being smug and complacent in its sporting and social hold over the towns already in its grip. The townsfolk had nowhere else to go on a Saturday afternoon, there were few other topics of conversation than Rugby League, and the special and sporting revolutions of the 1970s were a long way off. Rugby League was by choice parochial and isolated but maintained in apparent good health by the vibrancy within the northern towns and cities. That isolation was further engineered by the way the code has, somewhat amusingly, had to labour under the smear of professionalism. I use the word 'smear' deliberately for that is how the League code was considered by many.

The very people who frequent Wimbledon for the annual lawn tennis championships, with colossal amounts of prize money at stake for individual players, also go to Twickenham for the Five Nations championships. Yet the people who praise the sport which rewards a McEnroe or a Lendl or a Steffi Graf with tens of thousands of pounds, can criticise a game for making modest part-time payments to its players. Saatchi and Saatchi could not have done a better job over the years to render one product socially inferior on the flimsiest of theories regarding the supposed supremacy of the amateur ethos. These two attitudes have proved in the past strange obstacles to Rugby League's progress but their contribution to RL's failure to expand the game must not be exaggerated. The real reason for Union's expansion and, until recently, the stagnation of League, at any rate at professional level, has been the failure of the Rugby League hierarchy to take advantage of the quirks in our educational system, both pre-war and in the immediate post-war period.

The original breakaway from the Rugby Union in 1895 was to serve the interests of the miners, glassworkers and other manual labourers who needed to be given 'broken-time payments' to compensate for their hours off work while playing Rugby Union. In such a social grouping of its players and followers lay the basic problem which has until recently bedevilled Rugby League's expansion. Once the early administrators, who significantly had added Australia and New Zealand to the League family by 1908, had passed away, the League code suffered because of the limited educational opportunities offered to its followers. The split in education between the independent public schools which cultivated the supposedly socially superior Union code, the grammar schools which aped the public schools in their sporting ethos and outlook, and the secondary modern schools which, in the northern towns, adopted the League code, was to prove a disaster. Little attempt was made by the Rugby League authorities to promote the game within the public schools or the grammar schools, which until the 1970s remained the bastions of Rugby Union.

The modern critics who cite the all-embracing word

'image' and the lack of marketing consultants for the failure of League's international expansion would do well to remember that at least three countries, America (1947), Canada (1929) and Fiji (1913), had all taken up the Union code long before such arguments were advanced. That sort of expansion at the expense of RL bears witness to the stranglehold which the Union code has had on the upper reaches of our school system.

Whenever pupils left Harrow, Dulwich, or Rugby to further their careers abroad, for their relaxation they played the games learned in their younger days at school. As they became involved in the public and private affairs of countries like South Africa, Singapore, or Hong Kong, as the dominant figures in that area they encouraged the local population to join them in their favourite sports. Union thus made an immense impact abroad. Sadly for Rugby League most of the game's followers, on leaving their secondary modern schools in the north, moved into local industry at a time when industry in the north welcomed them. The mines, the mills, the glassworks, and the local councils retained the adherents of the League code while few had the intellectual or social passports to dominate abroad. Hence, the League code, by virtue of its followers' restricted career opportunities, remained exceptionally strong within its own base, pushing Rugby Union out to the very periphery of spectator and player involvement. But, beyond its narrow confines, other than in France where involvement with professionalism in the late 1930s saw whole sections of Rugby Union turn to League, Union has held sway and until recently has increased its hold. Only in Papua New Guinea, which mounted their first UK tour against British professional clubs in 1987, have we seen the Union method of expansion applied to League, and with such results that Rugby League is now that country's national sport.

In 1949, in Port Moresby, the Papuan capital, the first of six League matches kicked off between a team of civil servants working for the Australian government and another team drawn from the local banking and business community. As with Union's development overseas, so the Australians played the sport they had learned at school – Rugby League. Hence, as the devotees of League wielded influence in the country, so others of the local population joined them with the result that the following for Rugby League is now fanatical there. One had only to be present at Port Moresby for the Papua New Guinea v. Great Britain Test in 1988, watching the crowds locked outside listening to transistor radios with others sitting in trees to gain a vantage point, to appreciate the impact achieved by those early pioneers of forty years ago; and all achieved without that overused word 'marketing'.

The changes in schools during the past twenty-five years, the broadening outlook of the public and the sheer dogged determination on the part of amateur Rugby League have reversed the trend. At last Rugby League is taking up the challenge for the future, albeit rather like a relay runner who, as he clutches the baton, sees his opponent careering round the next bend. We have seen how the decline of the grammar school has had a profound effect on the strength and progress of Rugby Union. Rugby League, the preserve of the secondary modern, did not suffer so dramatically in the change to comprehensive schooling, except in so far as all team sports have declined. With the increase in comprehensive schools in the 1970s we have seen, in the state sector, lads emerging who have no wish to discriminate against the League game and who have never embraced Rugby Union. In other words, Rugby League is at last beginning to reach for the first time the 16- to 18-year-olds who will go on to enjoy some form of higher education. They form a group of students who, in the short period since 1982, have been in the vanguard of Rugby League's success story in universities, polytechnics and sixth-form colleges.

Rugby League moved quickly in the north of England to fill the team-sports vacuum often to be found in the new sixth-form colleges by forming the British Upper Schools and Colleges Amateur Rugby League Association (BUSCARLA), an umbrella body incorporated since 1987 in the English Schools RL. And, encouraged by outstanding success in an inaugural year which saw upwards of twenty-five colleges in membership, it was soon welcoming many of the more traditional Union-playing schools like my own.

In 1983 I was instrumental in including Rugby League in the games curriculum at Cowley, which had produced such Union internationals as Jack Heaton, Dickie Guest, Alan Ashcroft, Alan Brown, John Horton and myself, as well as over seventeen schoolboy internationals, during the past twenty-two years. This daring decision, taken after consulting over 400 prominent Old Cowleians, produced immediate playing success on the field when the school won the British Sixth-form Colleges Cup final at Headingley in 1984. Three of the boys were to accompany the BUSCARLA tour to Australia that summer, a tour from which has since emerged outstanding professional talent in Shaun Edwards (Wigan) and Paul Hulme (Widnes).

The experiment with League has now been extended to all the junior teams at Cowley with the result that youngsters between the ages of 11–16 years are now taking part in the local St Helens schools and national cup competitions with relish. Indeed the division of the rugby season into two periods from September to February, when most of the Union games are played, and from mid-February to May when the major League competitions take place, has admirably suited both staff and pupils. Considerable expense, too, is saved since the bulk of all League fixtures in the junior age-groups are played against schools within St Helens or other neighbouring towns as distinct from having to travel many miles to fulfil a Union fixture against a school, which, because it was once a grammar school, is the only Union-playing school in that area. The playing of both codes alongside each other has given staff and pupils much enjoyment, allowed lads with different playing styles or physiques to find success in one or other of the two codes, and has allowed a player to make up his own mind about his future preference at club level. Some England Schools Union players, like Jeff Rignall, have, in recent seasons, opted for Liverpool/St Helens Rugby Union club and Lancashire Under-21s while others, like John Fazackerley, have decided upon a career in professional Rugby League with Salford.

Sadly, the momentum gained by BUSCARLA in the mid 1980s has not been sustained in Yorkshire where there is now a definite need for a resurgence of interest; nor has the pioneer spirit, so evident in the early stages, taken League development into sixth-form colleges outside the north of England. This must be a future priority of the amateur Rugby League development officers for such colleges have no traditions of loyalty to one particular sport. Sport there is often organised by the students themselves, many of whom are only too keen to try their hand at a new game, and there is no headmaster resistance to the playing of League. In the more traditional League areas, Winstanley College, John Rigby College, Carmel College (formerly West Park Grammar School), Widnes Sixth-form College, and De La Salle College, for example, all once exclusively Union-playing schools, are now competing regularly in the thirteen-a-side code. And horizons for such teams and their players are always unlimited as can be seen from Wigan College's tour of Australia in the summer of 1988.

With Rugby League now breaking into the curriculum in once virgin territory at Bolton, Barrow, and Bury Sixth-form Colleges they and others like them are providing an enormous boost to that other area of education once taboo to League, the universities, polytechnics, and colleges of higher education. The sixth-form colleges must be the first stop on the Rugby League production line and the realm of higher education the finishing stage. From the universities and polytechnics will come men and perhaps women prepared to play their part on Rugby League's behalf in the world of business, the media, public relations, and even politics in the way that similar recruits have done for the Union code over the past ninety years.

I well remember a telephone call I made in the final week of September 1961 which convinced me that I had to go back to Leeds University for a further year to gain my postgraduate certificate of education. That telephone call was in response to a letter I had received from the Principal of Loughborough Colleges, which had indicated that few opportunities would be given me to play Rugby League at Loughborough. In the previous month I had signed for St Helens Rugby League club and wanted to go on combining my studies and rugby as I had done for the previous three years at Leeds University. Despite the Principal wishing me a 'happy and profitable year at Loughborough' at the end of his letter, the earlier tone indicated that whatever obstacles there were in the way of a Union player at Loughborough would not be removed in my case.

> Dear French,
>
> I was very sorry to learn from your letter that you have become a Rugby League Professional as we all would have been happier had you been free during the coming year to concentrate on your work and to help the Colleges in their Rugby Union matches.

> You will appreciate, I am sure, that we get many requests from students for leave of absence to play in representative and club matches of all kinds and that we have had to make fairly rigid rules about this in an effort to be fair to everyone. Leave of absence to a reasonable extent is given to those whose work is satisfactory and who are invited to play for Loughborough Colleges and the Universities Athletic Union in internationals and certain county matches but beyond that we cannot go so that you will only be able to play for St Helens when doing so does not involve absence from lectures or practical work here.

How times have changed! In 1988 Loughborough University won the Universities Athletic Union Rugby League championship for the third successive season by defeating Hull University at Featherstone. Indeed Loughborough University, the South Glamorgan Institute of Higher Education and my own alma mater, Leeds University, are now in the vanguard of the expansion of Rugby League in universities, polytechnics, and colleges. From humble beginnings at Liverpool and Leeds Universities in 1968, between whom the first ever university League match was played, such has been the growth in numbers attracted to RL, not only with northern ex-patriots from the blossoming sixth-form colleges but with students from all over the British Isles, that they have given the game at student level a truly national flavour.

With over thirty-four educational establishments now playing the game regularly, a glance at the successful sides in recent seasons reveals the strength of student rugby well away from the once traditional northern boundaries. West London Institute of Higher Education have won the British Colleges Cup final, and Newcastle Polytechnic have been runners-up in the British Polytechnic Trophy. But perhaps the most important advance in recent seasons has been the formation of Welsh and Scottish student representative teams for their inaugural match at St Helens in 1988; and the continued development at our two premier seats of learning, Oxford and Cambridge Universities.

The diverse backgrounds of many of the students representing Scotland in that first historic clash is yet further proof of the social progress now being made by the game at our major educational establishments. Few expected to find, in the Scottish team, Lord Dominic Addington, the youngest member of the House of Lords, Nick Harris, the captain of the Scottish Universities Rugby Union team, or John Pawson, who has represented the North and Midlands in Scottish representative Rugby Union. But they, and many more like them, lined up at St Helens. It was especially significant that the bulk of the Welsh players hailed from the South Glamorgan Institute which has been the premier breeding ground for Welsh international Union players, including Clive Griffiths, the current Welsh students League coach.

The annual Oxford v. Cambridge University League match, now heading for its tenth season, also continues to illustrate the startling advances made since those early formative days in 1980 when the open hostility of many in both universities, paltry grants, and the need to search out local authority pitches gave the pioneering students the incentive to survive. Not only have they survived but, especially at Cambridge, they have prospered and now attract recruits from as far afield as Uppingham, Harrow, Marlborough, Stowe and even from South Africa, New Zealand and the Middle East. The 'free gangway' of players between the two rugby codes has also eased the way for full Rugby Union Blues like John Risman, son of the ex-League and Union international Bev Risman, and

James Dingemans to play their part in two university matches. Such has been their success that Cambridge University, under the captaincy of Jamie Woodward, a Ph.D. at Darwin College, have recently made an ambitious tour of Australia, playing their counterparts in Sydney, Newcastle, and Toowoomba. Even Ian Williams, seven times capped by the Australian Rugby Union side, was persuaded to represent Oxford in the 1989 RL university match. And he was rewarded for his efforts by scoring the winning try in Oxford's 12–9 win.

As we approach the 1990s, student Rugby League is truly international and all the signs point to even further expansion. The visits of Hull University to play matches in Holland, the regular international fixtures between Great Britain and France and the ambitious Students World Cup, held in August of 1989 and based on the city of York, are all incentives for any young student, arriving for his Freshers weekend at the beginning of the new academic year, to play Rugby League. The introduction of sides from Holland and Ireland to the Students World Cup is further proof that the frontiers of student rugby are being rolled back.

Now there is an urgent need to consolidate the gains made and to expand the game at amateur level in these new territories. The workload of organising the League game, however, has increased to such an extent that it is doubtful if volunteers can continue to carry out these administrative burdens. Surely now is the time for the appointment of a development officer whose sole prerogative is the cultivation and administration of student Rugby League.

In any event, barriers to progress have been destroyed, and no student can say that he is unable to play the game. Moreover, the young League players now emerging from their universities, polytechnics, and colleges will doubtless include a future friendly banker, generous sponsor, or influential media figure for a thankful Rugby League. Those who remember fondly the sport of their youth will look kindly towards the needs of that sport. And departure from his seat of learning need not necessarily be the end of the young man's contact with the game should he take up a career in the south of England, the Midlands, or Wales. Many are now helping to swell the ranks of clubs like Hornsey in London, Hemel Hempstead in Hertfordshire and in the west country and Wales, all of which are waiting to greet them. Under the guidance of Bob Brown, a schoolmaster, the Hemel Hempstead club has progressed from a pub side in 1981 to a club with its own clubhouse, over 500 members and teams at every age-level. Bob Brown's proud boast is that in most years not a single northerner plays for the first team, such has been the influx of Rugby League resident players to the south of England. Hopefully in the near future ex-students will be added to his ranks.

It is accepted that Rugby League has crossed all social barriers at amateur level. But the professional game, too, is now regarded by many young men as a first-class social and financial complement to their normal career. Unlike soccer or cricket, where there has to be a full-time commitment, often damaging the promising careers of many well qualified teenagers, the semi-professionalism of Rugby League is highly attractive.

My good friend and predecessor on BBC television, Eddie Waring, regularly used to boast during his Saturday afternoon match commentaries that he could shout down a pit shaft of any colliery around Featherstone or Castleford and come up with half a dozen Rugby League forwards. Not any more. Changing social attitudes and the code's infiltration of the higher reaches of education have transformed the make-up of today's professional teams.

When I first signed for St Helens in August 1961 I joined a pack of forwards which was made up of two miners, a joiner, a lorry driver and a scrap metal merchant. Great fellows all, but what a difference there is today with regard to employment outside Rugby League.

The Wigan and Great Britain star, Joe Lydon, spent his formative years studying at Lancaster Polytechnic for his BA in graphic design, preparing for a career as an advertising consultant. The young Hull KR hooker, David Harrison, a history graduate of Lancaster University, has gained his MA following research into the conditions of the miners and glass-workers of St Helens between the wars – the very people who were traditionally the backbone of the town's Rugby League team.

Yes, in the words of Bob Dylan's old tune, 'the times they are a changing'. At last Rugby League is emerging as a sport which welcomes all classes within its ranks as players, spectators or administrators. It has tried to do so for the past ninety years without success and only as the sport nears its centenary can it truly say that it again embraces the social strata that it once did immediately before its breakaway from the Union code.

6

Worlds Apart

A reader glancing through the Rugby League results and casting his eye over his team's position in the two-division League set-up in any Monday morning newspaper probably has little idea of the startling contrasts between each of the thirty-four member clubs of the Rugby Football League. There can be few clubs in any organised sport with such contrasts in management, playing staff, facilities and finance, yet all seeking to promote the same aim – the furtherance of professional Rugby League football. Ranging from a life of five years to ninety-three, such clubs have experienced their successes and their failures but all, the occasional hiccup apart, have maintained their existence. The question to be asked is whether the present mixture of clubs, all treated equally by the League management body and left to find their own playing level within a two-division programme, will endure beyond the year 2000. I have my doubts, for changing social and economic conditions and the public's attitude will almost certainly press for further change and development.

The management structure of the clubs can vary from a tightly knit body of four powerful and wealthy directors, flanked by a large body of shareholders, as at Wigan, or an annually elected committee as at Widnes. Most of the clubs own their own grounds and there are few better appointed stadiums in the country than Headingley, Central Park, or Knowsley Road, the homes of Leeds, Wigan, and St Helens. Others, like Hunslet, share the ground at Elland Road, owned by the Leeds local authority, with the soccer club Leeds United. The trend for many clubs in the 1980s has been to introduce similar ground-sharing schemes with friendly soccer clubs.

Fulham, who now use a polytechnic ground at Chiswick, Carlisle, Cardiff and Kent Invicta (before the collapse of the last two clubs) were the first to initiate ground sharing. Many clubs, like Barrow and Rochdale Hornets, are now involved in moves to a council-owned stadium as the local authority begins to play an increasing role in the sporting affairs of the town and has hopes of making the Rugby League club the focal point for sport in a multi-sport municipal stadium. As in soccer, such clubs exist in large or small conurbations where the potential for spectators is greater or smaller and where the financial fund-raising possibilities can be so disproportionate. Hence, some clubs always have the potential for success around them; for others, their very existence will always be a struggle with only limited hopes for the future. Yet all clubs, successful or not, rich or poor, old-established or fledgeling newcomers, are thrown together under the same playing structure in the two divisions of the Rugby Football League.

A look at the structure, outlook, and potential of two clubs at the top and bottom of those two divisions – Wigan and Mansfield Marksman – will surely indicate the need for radical change in the League's structure and in the game's approach to professionalism.

Wigan RLFC was founded by a group from the local cricket club on 21 November 1872. The club's profits of £2.0.3 in that inaugural season of 1872–73 might seem tiny when compared to the figure of £130,000 for the 1985–86 season, a record for a Rugby League club, but from the start Wigan was always likely to become one of the great rugby clubs of the world.

That Wigan's fame should have been built on the League code was due to their representative's presence at the George Hotel in Huddersfield on that fateful night of 29 August 1895 when twenty-one of the northern-based Rugby Union clubs broke away to form the Northern Union and ultimately to develop the thirteen-a-side game. Throughout its history, Wigan has been in the vanguard of the League's progress and it did not take their administrators and players long to establish a world-wide reputation for the quality of their play. A glance at the honours boards mounted proudly on the wall alongside the entrance to the club indicates why Wigan can boast countless championship-winning sides and no less than nine Challenge Cup victories among the many other trophies won during their illustrious history. To this tiny mining town in South Lancashire have come some of the finest players in the world to parade their talents before an adoring public.

From Wales came Johnny Ring, Jim Sullivan, and Billy Boston to complement the native talents of Eric Ashton, Joe Egan, Ken Gee, Jimmy Leytham and Brian McTigue. South Africa has played a prominent part in the club's rise with Union converts such as Fred Griffiths, Adrian van Heerden, Ray Mordt, Rob Louw, and George van Rooyen joining the professional ranks. Australia has supplied the club with Hector Gee, Steve Ella, John Ferguson, Brett Kenny, and Greg Dowling while such Kiwis as Cec Mountford, Lance Todd, Charlie Seeling, and Brian Nordgren, have maintained New Zealand's reputation for producing quality players. Today, stars of the calibre of Joe Lydon, Ellery Hanley, and Andy Goodway are joined by such Kiwi internationals as Kevin Iro, Dean Bell, and Adrian Shelford to keep the 'cherry and whites' at the top of the Rugby League tree.

It is not without accident that the Wigan club is acknowledged throughout the world for its deeds on the field of play. Yet such are the ups and downs of sport that even this mighty club suffered ignominy at the end of the 1979–80 season when relegation to the second division had to be faced. The immediate future for Rugby League in Wigan looked bleak, despite a vast reservoir of support lying dormant. It needed an earthquake to jolt the club out of its apathy and its downward slide. One came along in the shape of the dynamic Maurice Lindsay, the owner of a plant hire company, whose huge earth-moving machines were used to remove large decaying bodies in their path. Such was Maurice Lindsay's task at Wigan.

As an occasional match sponsor, Maurice had already indicated more than passing interest in the Wigan club when, having watched their final home defeat against Leeds by 12–20 in that disastrous spring of 1980, he was invited to join the club's ten-man board along with his good friend Jack Robinson, a local antiques dealer. Though Wigan immediately gained promotion the following season after winning twenty of their twenty-eight matches and finishing runners-up to the second division champions York, both he and Jack Robinson could still see little future for a club faced with debts of £300,000. Advised by lawyers, they began work on a scheme which would enable them to take over the board and project Wigan to the top of world Rugby League. As Maurice Lindsay admits, 'We were getting nowhere with a twelve-man board. We used to argue from 6 p.m. to midnight about where we should buy the next wheelbarrow and what make it should be.' Finally, at a lively shareholders meeting, Lindsay aided by Robinson and Tom Rathbone, a local baker, put his ideas for the Wigan club to the vote, and, though the shareholders were retained as a positive influence within the club, the Rugby League's equivalent of the Social Democratic Party's 'gang of four' were firmly in control at Central Park when Jack Hilton, a long-serving director and an ex-international player, joined the instigators of the take over to complete the quartet. All dug deeply into their pockets and pledged sums of £150,000 to help allay the club's debts and provide a cash flow to enable Wigan to go forward without ever looking over its shoulder for pursuing creditors.

'Our greatest asset was the rugby-mad paying public of Wigan. We had to reawaken the giant but we had to progress slowly at first, step by step, in order to lay down a firm base from which eventually to launch ourselves to bigger things,' insists Maurice Lindsay, and indeed the shrewd rugby knowledge of the four directors stood the club in good stead.

Such experienced campaigners as Glyn Shaw, Alan Hodkinson and Gary Stephens were bought at modest fees to help the club's return to the first division and, when there, younger players like David Stephenson, Colin Whitfield, and Henderson Gill were added to consolidate their position. The giant had awakened and its revival in the 1980s, first under Alex Murphy, and then under the joint coaches, Alan McInnes and Colin Clarke, saw the John Player Trophy (twice) and the Challenge Cup return to Central Park. Great overseas stars added to the attraction as money became more easily available and the feats of Brett Kenny, John Ferguson, Steve Ella, and Greg Dowling helped to push Wigan's average gate beyond the 13,000 mark, a figure unimagined when attendances sank below 4000 in the second division. The arrival of the New Zealand Test coach, Graham Lowe, at the beginning of the 1986–87 season, heralded Wigan's greatest ever cup-winning success of four trophies in a season, eleven in three years, including the Challenge Cup. Now his decision, in May 1989, to rejoin his teenage daughters in Australia will leave a gap exceptionally difficult to fill.

The early Wigan pioneers would probably stare with incredulity at the club's balance sheet and its income and expenditure today. Great Britain's premier club needs a strong financial base if it is to maintain its standards. Sponsorship, as in most sports, is now the lifeblood of most Rugby League clubs and Wigan is no exception. A three-year contract with the Lancashire sports outfitters JJB, worth £100,000, and a similar deal with the locally based Heinz company has given financial stability to Central Park. Now a recently negotiated deal with the North-west Electricity Board, worth £250,000, has assured the club's future over the next two seasons. Not content with a £100,000 sponsorship deal, the Heinz company has also funded a new £46,000 electronic scoreboard on which every conceivable score, scorer, or message can be recorded. Further lucrative contracts with the sports goods companies, Puma and Umbro, for the supply of kit has placed the club on a similar footing to Everton in the soccer world. Nor does the input of sponsorship money end here for Wigan ensure that each match day is sponsored by a local company or individual. In return for an annual income of approximately £20,000 from this source, the sponsors and guests are treated to match tickets, cocktails, lunch and an after-match buffet. And there is no shortage of takers.

The commercial offices at the club are a hive of activity and there is ample work to keep four full-time employees fully occupied. Over £50,000 a season is now raised by the sale of replica Wigan jerseys, scarves, T-shirts, bob hats, souvenir mugs, flags, and so on, and, having taken over the job of securing their own ground advertising, there is plenty of scope here too for the staff. Advertising boards, strategically placed round the perimeter walls of the playing area, are a lucrative business at any major sports event and Wigan is reaping the benefit of handling this business itself. 'If we are featured on television on at least four occasions during the season, we will recoup another £100,000 from the sale of our advertising boards,' Maurice Lindsay proudly boasts.

When New Zealand's Test skipper, the 6 foot 5 inches and 16-stone prop, Graeme West, signed for Wigan in 1982 he probably would not have realised that, as well as captaining the club to glory on the field, he would occupy a full-time job rather like an entertainments officer at the club. Graeme's agreeable task is to organise over 2000 members into paying £2 a week into a central fund, out of which £100,000 profits accrue for buying new players. The members, known as the 'Knights of Central Park', in return for their payments are involved in weekly lotteries with cars, continental holidays and large sums of cash as prizes, as well as being invited to the many entertainments laid on by 'Uncle' Graeme West. In the Riverside club, a huge night-club built into the Wigan club complex, the members can enjoy fancy dress parties, sports evenings, magic shows for children, and Christmas parties all organised by Graeme and his willing band of helpers. Players, all of whom are required to take part in the activities, and spectators mingle together and a warm family atmosphere is generated. Mums, dads, and children become as much a part of the club as the highest paid player.

To provide for a full-time administrative staff of twelve, made up of four commercial officers, three secretaries and five ground maintenance workers, as well as a full-time coach in Graham Lowe and forty-two contracted players, the club obviously has to generate considerable income. However, when a season's gate receipts, from an average crowd approaching 14,000 a match, are added to all of Wigan's fund-raising schemes their income is well in excess of £1m a season. That is a staggering sum by any sporting standards, which Wigan's 'gang of four' invest in their already palatial facilities to provide even greater comfort for the supporters and even greater successes on the field.

In recent seasons visitors to Central Park will have seen the new floodlights, checked the score on the new electronic scoreboard, and, even in the depths of an icy winter, will have enjoyed a match played by courtesy of the underground heating. Already, however, there are further plans to upgrade the ground with extensions to the grandstands to provide seating for 10,000 supporters, alongside a further 28,000 standing places. To cater for modern tastes luxury executive boxes will be built in the main stand. This is a far cry from the old 'cloth cap and muffler' image of Rugby League. A steakhouse is also to be built alongside the Riverside Suite where spectators will be able to book a pre- or post-match meal and which can be used as a pleasant mid-week restaurant for the fans.

The controversial dismissal of the likeable joint coaches Colin Clarke and Alan McInnes at the close of the 1985–86 season, despite their successful cup wins, heralded the arrival of the Kiwi, Graham Lowe. Already a respected name in international League circles for his successes at Test level with the New Zealand team, he had an awesome task in front of him to maintain Wigan's steady upward climb. His appointment as the only full-time manager–coach in the game, a trend later followed by Leeds with the appointment of the ex-Great Britain coach, Maurice Bamford, and in the 1988–89 season by Hull, Castleford, and Halifax ensured that he had the time to plan his campaign. Indeed Graham expressed his delight at this new found freedom for coaching by observing, 'How I coached New Zealand while being the sales director of

1. Ray French – as BBC television's
Rugby League commentator.

2. The Great Britain Rugby League squad of 1948 in training before the first Test against Australia. *Left to right, standing:* Ken Gee (Wigan), Bob Nicholson (Huddersfield), George Curran (Salford), Stan McCormick (St Helens), Willie Horne (Barrow), David Valentine (Huddersfield), Jimmy Ledgard (Leigh), Albert Pimblett (Warrington), John Lawrenson (Wigan), Trevor Foster (Bradford Northern), Jim Featherstone (Warrington), Ernest Ward (Bradford Northern): *left to right, kneeling:* Gerry Helme (Warrington), Joe Egan (Wigan), Russell Pepperell (Workington).

3. Ray French was an outstanding Rugby Union coach for Lancashire Schools and is still in command of both codes of rugby at Cowley School. Here, at half-time, he exhorts his Cowley School side to even greater efforts in their match, which they won, against Randwick High School during their Australian tour of 1981.

4. Alan Prescott (St Helens) was Great Britain's captain on the 1958 tour of Australia. Though his arm had been broken during the first half of the second Test in 1958 he refused to leave the field and led his team to an heroic victory. On his day, Prescott was probably the fastest prop forward in the game and easily wins a place in Ray's 1946–61 team.

5. Trevor Foster (Bradford Northern) played in all three of Northern's Cup final appearances between 1947–49 after playing Rugby Union for Newport. He wins a place in Ray's 1946–61 team on the strength of his prolific try-scoring ability.

6. Dick Huddart (St Helens), picked by Ray for his 1961–72 side, was a strong running forward from Cumbria whose job was to break tackles and then sprint thirty or forty yards to the try-line. Huddart later played with distinction for the St George club in Sydney.

7. Vince Karalius (Widnes) holds high the Challenge Cup after Widnes had beaten Hull KR at Wembley in 1964. Karalius wins a place in Ray's 1961–72 side as a legendary no. 13 whose strong surging runs and devastating tackling during Great Britain's 1958 tour of Australia earned him the nickname of 'the wild bull of the pampas'.

8. Ellery Hanley (Wigan), an outstanding example of a modern loose forward, easily wins a place in Ray's 1981–88 team.

9. Martin Offiah (Widnes), another member of Ray's 1981–88 team, is gifted with pure speed, a devastating swerve, and a determination to score tries. Here he touches down another of the sixty tries he scored during the 1988–89 season, this time against Salford with Adrian Hadley arriving too late to get his man.

10. Mal Meninga, the great Australian centre, whom Ray helped to secure for St Helens during the summer of 1984.

11. David Campese, the brilliant Australian wing threequarter, is one of the few players guaranteed to draw the crowds in Rugby Union today.

12. *Left* Ian Williams, blessed with devastating pace, had been capped several times by Australia before winning his Blue at Oxford during the 1988–89 season. He then played for Oxford in the university Rugby League match at Headingley, before gaining another Union cap for Australia against the British Lions in July 1989.

13. *Above* Alan Tait (Widnes), capped by Scotland Rugby Union as a centre, is now the best attacking full-back in RL and won the man-of-the-match award in the 1989 Premiership final against Hull.

14. Another convert from Rugby Union during the 1988–89 season was the Tongan Emosi Koloto who had an outstanding first season with Widnes Rugby League club.

15. Lee Crooks (Leeds, formerly Hull) made his debut for Great Britain in 1982 at the age of eighteen. He is picked for Ray's 1981–88 team as a superb ball distributor, a skill which probably accounts for his world record transfer fee of £172,000 when he left Hull for Leeds. Crooks has also played in Australia with Western Suburbs and Balmain.

two companies, I'll never know.' However, a glimpse at a sample of Wigan's early season training schedules indicates the thoroughness and eye for detail practised by Lowe at Central Park during his three years as coach.

His plans for the 1987–88 season were first hatched in the May of that year when, after discussions with his assistants, the A team coach Terry Cassidy, the Colts coach John Grady, the fitness co-ordinator Bill Hartley, and the training co-ordinator Geoff Hurst, a pre-season summer training programme was devised for all the playing staff. Following the accepted practice of Australian Rugby League all the players were required to be at a certain level of fitness by 20 June 1987, after working strenuously at their individual fitness training schedules. Much of the designated programme, according to Graham Lowe, 'revolves round running, agility work, and weight training', and is similar for most players but, as an indicator of the coaching staff's awareness of each player's deficiencies, individual programmes are also suggested. Steve Hampson, hoping that season to secure the Great Britain full-back position, was outlined a weight-training schedule for the summer months, which would increase his upper body bulk yet at the same time increase his speed. His first appearance at training and his superb performances in the Charity Cup match against Halifax which preceded the league programme testified to its value. Shaun Edwards, the talented and precocious Great Britain half-back, also worked to increase his upper body strength, while Joe Lydon, the scorer of that never-to-be-forgotten seventy yards try against Australia in the first Test of 1986 at Old Trafford, was surprisingly instructed to work at his speed off the mark and encouraged to achieve sustained explosive power running. The cheeky scrum-half, Andy Gregory, spent a quieter summer working on his chip kicks, so vital a skill in breaking up a tight defence.

Once I had forced my way past a gaggle of young girls gathered at the club entrance, eager for a glimpse of their Sunday afternoon heroes, I was surprised to see the extent of the activity at 6 o'clock on a Tuesday evening, an early start for Rugby League clubs. Already Geoff Hurst, the co-ordinator who arranges the mechanics of the weekly training sessions both at Central Park and at Robin Park, a council-owned sports complex, was shuttling busily between the rooms which adjoin the central corridor of the club, a corridor leading directly to the playing pitch. Geoff had by now received the mandatory telephone calls from any players who were going to be late or missing from training, had briefed the coaches and players and, with Mike Callaghan, the physiotherapist, had already indicated which players needed treatment. Andy Gregory sat like a miniature Buddha atop the bench, electric pads strapped to his chest, as one of the many modern gadgets scattered around the medical room eased his rib injury from the previous match. The young hooker, Martin Dermott, sitting quietly alongside Gregory, received treatment on his injured knee ligaments from the probing hands of Mike Callaghan who faced the prospect of an easy night with only two or three other customers waiting.

Though Tuesday, Thursday, and Friday nights or Saturday morning are the regular training times most players will have trained another couple of nights by themselves or availed themselves of the well appointed weights room alongside the dressing-rooms. The players are keen to be fit and Graham Lowe was quick to dispel any doubts one may have about the British Rugby League players' acceptance of his arduous regime: 'In Australia and New Zealand people are brainwashed by the media about the so-called bad habits of Englishmen, but I have found the situation to be the total opposite. We have no problems with our playing staff.' And Steve Hampson, the young full-back from the Vulcan Rugby Union club at Newton-le-Willows, bore testimony to those sentiments for he had already been on the training pitch behind the Kop end of the Central Park ground for fully forty minutes before training started. He and the conditioner, Bill Hartley, the ex-European Games athlete, were hard at work developing a rhythm and a high step in Hampson's running style in order to increase his speed when joining the attack from full-back.

Bill Hartley, whom Graham Lowe believes has 'a unique understanding of rugby players', was first asked to harness his considerable coaching skills to Rugby League by his friend, Vince Karalius, when the latter was coach at Widnes in the 1983–84 season. Confessing to being 'very surprised at the physical demands of the game', Bill's task, as well as conditioning the players, is to adapt his knowledge of sprinting to the demands of Rugby League. Both he and Graham Lowe concentrate heavily on sprint work, even with the prop forwards, for, as Bill explains, 'The basics of running can desert a player who is trailing through six inches of mud on a wet pitch in December and January.' Steve Hampson, relaxed and smiling, certainly enjoyed the benefits of such individual tuition as he paced the length of the training pitch with Bill Hartley alongside, coaxing him to the right rhythm and lift of his legs necessary to increase speed.

Once the training evening was under way the players, under the careful scrutiny of Bill, twisted, stretched, and bent their limbs in all manner of exercises for fully fifteen minutes so as not to risk the possibility of a pulled muscle or of aggravating an old injury. As with all rugby players friendly banter was the order of the evening with Andy Gregory, now released from the physiotherapist's table, strutting around the pitch like Popeye with sleeves tightly rolled up, chest sticking out, and commenting mercilessly on any or all of the players. A new £40,000 signing from Salford, Ged Byrne, feels the friendly lash of his tongue as Gregory spots the large size of Byrne's new boots. 'You'll never fall over in them, Ged. You want to rent out advertising boards on them for Sundays.' Ged Byrne grins, content to be accepted at once within the camaraderie of the squad, but concentrates on his exercises.

On most Tuesday evenings throughout the season all the forty-two contracted staff as well as the amateur Colts players come together as one large group in an effort to instil correct techniques throughout all playing levels of the club. The players are divided into four teams or groups under a captain appointed by Graham Lowe and take part in a series of games, training routines, and conditioning exercises; points are awarded to each team for their performances. Points will also be added for a team's attitude, discipline, and promptness in performance at training so that an air of keen competition runs right through the club. Over each four-week period all manner of skills in handling, passing, tackling, running, and set-piece play are dealt with before the teams, rather in the manner of a house system at school, earn their prizes. All this activity is not at a peak of intensity every week, for as Graham Lowe indicates, 'We build up a season in peaks and troughs. Some weeks we will be very low key, when we are just ticking over deliberately, but in other weeks we will exert pressure as we build up to important matches.'

But whatever is the intensity of training on a Tuesday evening all three coaches will be overseeing the performances of each of his teams under the direction of Graham Lowe. All are thirsting for new ideas and Lowe ensures that the players are made to think deeply about their sport and gain a sense of responsibility by his insisting that, 'the forwards as well as the backs come up with a move every week for the coaching staff to consider.'

The division of the players into the three distinct playing squads, first team, Alliance, and Colts, takes place on a Thursday evening to allow the coaches to work on the teams for the coming weekend matches. Though each coach is given complete freedom to plan and organise his training session as he wishes, all work under a set pattern for the club is laid down by Graham Lowe. 'All staff are aware of our team plans for matches, but we never stifle flair and individuality. We encourage it within the framework of our team plans. In the 1986–87 season we created a record points scoring total for Rugby League with 941 points and we produced the best defensive system in the game by conceding only 193 points – a sure sign of individual brilliance and team planning.' Lowe insists that all his players plan for a particular match for, as he believes, 'Planning gives confidence to a player. It is an ally for him to fall back on when things go wrong during a match. But we never stifle flair, rather the opposite. I always urge Ellery Hanley, Andy Gregory, or Joe Lydon to do their own thing.'

Lowe and Geoff Hurst put their thinking and planning into practice when a typical Thursday training session gets under way. Once Hartley has toned up the squad, Graham Lowe might begin with a period of defensive work for the back unit with Lowe himself filling a huge gap in the midfield line-up where the forwards are expected to be. Moving continuously up and down the field and rolling the ball in the direction of a particular player, kicking it, or hurling it forward he will make sure that the backs align properly and approach the imaginary attacking side with alacrity; he also checks on the positional play of the wings as they are expected to cover the kick anticipated on the sixth tackle. Meanwhile Geoff Hurst allows the club captain, Graeme West, to take control of the forwards in their practices round the play-the-ball situation, coaxing them verbally through endless performances of the unit skill and countless ploys around it. After a time the backs halt their defensive practices and, before joining with the forwards for a series of rehearsals of various kick-offs or restarts in play, they practise high speed passing and running. As the Kiwi Test centre, Dean Bell, hurtles from depth onto the short passes of Shaun Edwards or runs parallel to the touchlines onto a long ball floated delicately in his direction by Andy Gregory, Graham Lowe moves alongside quietly offering advice.

During the couple of hours of training, any strain or slight injury problem which might be giving trouble is attended to on the training pitch by Mike Callaghan or the player is sent inside to the physiotherapist's room for further, more intense, treatment. On warm, early season evenings Mike Callaghan's task also is to be on hand with a large flask of Gatorade, a thirst quenching drink favoured by American Footballers, which replaces the potassium and sodium lost during training. The players are not allowed to drink for too long during training.

Bill Hartley urges the players to be careful with their alcohol consumption, and cigarette smoking is actively discouraged. Watching the players consume large quantities of pasties and chips or pie and peas prepared by the kitchen staff after every training session I agree with Bill Hartley who says, 'We discourage the lads from indulging in any of the gimmick diets or the latest fashionable food fads.'

The final official training session on a Friday evening or a Saturday morning is naturally given over to preparation for the weekend fixture and, as might be expected, the concentration is on the team as a unit and on the plan for the match. Every aspect of the game is discussed and worked on whether it be in defence or attack, at set-piece or in loose play, at the kick-offs or on receipt of the ball from restarts. Again, for a couple of hours, Graham Lowe insists that the team 'practise for every eventuality, which might occur in the match and work accordingly on all phases of the game'. A great believer in giving players increased responsibility and trying to make them more aware of the demands of Rugby League as a whole, Lowe will show videos of previous matches or of future opposition to highlight his side's faults or an opponent's weaknesses. Lectures are held periodically during the season on an aspect like scrummaging with every player obliged to speak on his performance in the previous match. This is a most unnerving experience, even for the most hardy professional, but provides a salutary lesson when the coaches have added their comments.

Though there is a full programme of training exercises and routines to suit each of the players, they are also trained specifically for the roles they can perform. The expectations from Brian Case at prop are different from those of Kevin Iro in the centre but all are expected, in Graham Lowe's words, 'to have the same attitude and the same commitment to the Wigan club'. That attitude even extends to the morning of the match and a routine that many of my contemporaries or even myself would have blanched at in the 1960s. For the present-day Wigan players there is no extra hour in bed on a Sunday morning prior to the match in the afternoon. No, a jog for a couple of miles or a few sprints is the order of the morning so that, according to Bill Hartley, 'their pulse and heart rate rise so that their body becomes attuned for when they first run in the match. It prevents a sluggish start, just like a car starting up on a cold morning. Keep the pulse rate high and the player will kick off in top gear.' I'll believe you, Bill!

For those players who hold down a full-time job the weekly time-table of a Rugby League player can be a most demanding one. The rewards, however, as at Wigan, can ease the pain. Indeed, the scale of the rewards available these days to a player like Joe Lydon, who is good enough to spend British summers in Australia on an additional lucrative contract with the Australian club, Eastern Suburbs, means his earnings will be comparable to many first division soccer players.

The average first-team player at Wigan will have signed a contract for a period of one, two, or three years for a retainer of around £5000 a year, though the top Great Britain stars will be paid much more than that. On top of the basic contractual payments a Wigan player might have earned £1200 for winning the John Player Cup final in 1986–87, £750 for the Lancashire Cup final, and £2500 if the club had won the only trophy to elude them that season, the Silk Cut Challenge Cup. In the following season the players' reward for bringing home the Challenge Cup was in fact £3000. In a typical season of league and cup matches all players have, in win bonuses, the opportunity to earn a figure as high as £30,000. That is not bad for a part-time sport. Some like Ellery Hanley, Andy Gregory, or Andy Goodway can double that figure or even treble it by guesting with an Australian club in the summer.

With such financial inducements to the players, and with a galaxy of talent and newly emerging stars providing such an attraction on the pitch, it is surely inconceivable that Wigan will ever again sink to the second division. Such now are the resources of the club and such is the volume of public support through the turnstiles at Central Park that the lesser clubs can only admire from afar. Whether they be an original founder member of the League code in 1895, like Batley, or a new entrant during the expansion of the 1980s, like Mansfield Marksman, some of these smaller clubs have to struggle to keep themselves alive. In the case of Mansfield Marksman it has been the dogged determination of a group of dedicated individuals which keeps the Rugby League flag flying over the Midlands.

Any player, sales representative, or potential sponsor wanting to meet David Parker, the managing director of Mansfield Marksman, has no need to travel to Mansfield, where they do not play, nor to Alfreton, a small town nearby, where they used to play, nor to the Harvey Hadden Stadium, Nottingham, where they do now play. He should seek out a neat semi-detached house in a pleasant residential suburb of Halifax and step gingerly towards Mr Parker's office. Having carefully avoided the line of Mansfield Marksman jerseys, shorts, and stockings drying in the kitchen, the visitor should not be tempted to sample the huge mound of ham sandwiches, meat pies, orange squash, and the accompanying brown sauce bottle which David's wife Elizabeth is packing into a large brown cardboard box. All the contents, when transported by David to the Hipperholme and Hinchcliffe High School playing-fields for the players at the end of their evening training session, will be carefully counted by the hungry players in the event of a lost pie. David's young daughter, Charlotte, suitably clad in a miniature Mansfield jersey and clutching a teddy which also sports a faded jumper in the team's colours, helps the visitor to manoeuvre himself round the boxes of first-aid material, rugby balls, and spare programmes piled high in the hallway. A knock at the office door, or rather the dining-room, will reveal the hub of the Mansfield Marksman club.

Seated behind a mound of raffle tickets, tote lottery tickets, empty wage packets, souvenir brochures, and advertising leaflets, David Parker attends to the day-to-day running of the club, unpaid of course. Whether it be washing kit, preparing meals, paying wages, signing players, or organising training, David and Elizabeth are at the helm. Though now helped by a four-man board of directors, mostly wisely recruited from within the east Midlands where the game must take root, it is to David Parker and his active chairman, Paul Tomlinson, that Mansfield owes its brief past and also, we hope, a long and strong future.

Evidence of the forty-year-old David Parker's infatuation with Rugby League can be deduced from his dismissal from work when, as a young apprentice draughtsman, he took time off to watch a BBC Floodlit Trophy match. In fact the sacking was not all that cruel, because for the past twenty-three years David has helped my predecessor Eddie Waring and myself behind the scenes with preparations for the BBC television commentaries where his enthusiasm has burned brightly. So brightly that, with a consuming ambition to control his own club and having tried to take over the then ailing Halifax in 1981, he helped to finance two experimental matches featuring Leigh and Carlisle in Grimsby in 1982 and Hull KR and Cardiff at Nottingham Forest in 1983. Though both ventures were inconclusive, in the crowd at Nottingham were Geoff Huckstep, an exiled Hull KR fan working for Nottingham City Council, Chris Worthington, a solicitor, and Paul Tomlinson, then a Derby County shareholder, all of whom approached David Parker with offers of help if he could generate interest elsewhere in the Midlands.

A stroke of luck or foresight led David to the Shay, the home of Halifax Town soccer club, to watch them play Mansfield Town on a Friday evening in the late August of 1983. A touch of cheek led him to knock on the door of the directors' room after the match and ask to speak to Richard Hartley, then the chairman of Mansfield Town. Bluntly asking Mr Hartley if he was interested in having a Rugby League club at Field Mill, David was taken aback when he replied that he was indeed interested in such a ground-sharing scheme. The door to the Rugby League was open for David, and following a meeting with the Mansfield Town board on 3 October 1983, having promised to form a four-man board of directors and pay a season's rent of £10,000, David Parker, Paul Tomlinson and company had their dreams realised at last. Mansfield Marksman entered the Rugby League for the start of the 1984–85 season.

Doubts were already being raised over the new club's ability to pay £10,000 ground rent and, despite topping the second division table by winning their opening nine games, the average of 1300 spectators a match that was needed to support that sort of cost was not forthcoming. David Parker admits, 'We put blinkers on ourselves for we were so desperate to start up the side, having at last got the offer of a good ground. It proved a costly mistake and was most damaging to our progress.' The situation looked bleak for the board and the nominee from Mansfield Brewery who agreed to sponsor the club in that initial season. In addition, the initial cost of assembling a side of mainly experienced professionals ensured that the Mansfield club faced a deficit of £93,000 at the end of its first playing season, and both David and Paul Tomlinson were being chased by a small band of irate creditors. The club was on the brink of failure as directors developed cold feet and departed, to leave Parker and Tomlinson faced with the prospect of injecting £7000 of their own money into the club to stave off bankruptcy.

However, at the beginning of the 1985–86 season the club moved to Alfreton soccer club, a team in the Northern Premier League with a tiny, compact ground with a capacity of 4000. It was to prove the club's saviour. The small stand, well appointed clubhouse and spacious changing-rooms were adequate for Mansfield's requirements, and the ground rent of £150 a match was a bargain. As Paul

Tomlinson confesses, 'Alfreton was an oxygen tent where the patient was recovering but, for overall good health, we still needed a city environment and we had to continue to promote the game in Mansfield.'

Indeed, Fulham's move from their original home at Craven Cottage to the present-day polytechnic stadium at Chiswick followed roughly the same course. High costs, a clash of interests with the soccer club, and too great a reliance on old professionals from the north almost cost Fulham, as it nearly did Mansfield, their very existence. Thankfully the changed circumstances at Fulham and their more realistic appraisal of future prospects has restored the club to better health. The same can be said of Mansfield whose deficit had been cut by roughly £68,000 within twelve months of uprooting themselves.

After two seasons at Alfreton, Marksman moved again, this time to Sutton Town FC at Kirkby-in-Ashfield. There the dedicated band of workers faced a truly uphill task, as they tried to generate the revenue needed to lift the club. Though that ground lay only three miles from Mansfield city centre the directors decided to move once again for the 1989-90 season to the Harvey Hadden Stadium in Nottingham and assumed the name of Nottingham City.

Against a run of poor performances, winning only two out of fifty-two games before coach Jim Crellin and his assistant Ray Clarke arrived halfway through the 1986–87 season, the average match attendance had dropped to a mere 381 spectators. That sort of crowd may seem derisory but is still commonplace at many Rugby Union clubs, such as New Brighton, Roundhay, and Rosslyn Park, and to my mind is acceptable at new League clubs so long as the income generated makes the club viable. Average yearly gate receipts of £10,000 for Mansfield Marksman was helped by an annual £10,000 sponsorship of the club by the Mansfield Brewery and a further £1000 receipts from the advertising boards round the pitch. Television payments, levy payments from Rugby League central funds, and payments from sponsored cup events, such as the Challenge Cup, bring in another £11,000 over a season.

However, the bonus for the club in the first four years of its existence was the work of Bob Fox, the former Bentley and Yarborough amateur Rugby League secretary, who had also been secretary of the short-lived club Kent Invicta. Bob, the only full-time employee of the club, attended to the fund-raising ventures, and raised about £10,000 a year through the sale of raffle tickets, bingo tickets, programme advertising and social events – work which was vital to the club's solvency and which gave people an awareness of the club in and around Alfreton. With an income approaching £42,000 a year, less than Wigan's income from the sale of mugs, jerseys, and souvenirs, it was no wonder that David Parker had to organise the occasional auction of Rugby League memorabilia in a local amateur club to raise £136 coach fees for an away match. The hardworking band of supporters who control the turnstiles on Sundays on a voluntary basis also planned, and still do, social events to help with travel costs rather in the style of the self-help practised by most amateur Rugby Union clubs.

Despite the struggles, the stress, and the heartaches, 'the thrill of sitting at the front of the coach when we pull onto the forecourt at Wigan or pass through the gates at Headingley, Leeds, knowing your team is sat behind you, is worth it all,' insists David Parker. The humorous moments, too, provide David and his directors with an occasional lift. 'We represented the Rugby League against the Catalan XIII at Perpignan in what proved to be a very rough match. Three of our players were carried to the hospital across the road, each one to the accompaniment of the band playing the Dead March. I had to pay 45 francs a stitch for gut out of my own pocket at the hospital. The club couldn't afford the hospital fees.' Whatever the fun, the players, coaches, and directors treat the game as seriously as their counterparts at Wigan, some possibly more so as they strain to emulate Wigan, only with significant differences. The money available, the quality of the playing staff, and the time available for coaching are all constraints, but in the 1987–88 season, Mansfield's most successful year, the coaches Jim Crellin and Ray Clarke went about their duties in a busy and disciplined way.

Jim Crellin, during the day a safety officer with Manchester City Council and an ex-professional player of eleven years with Workington, Oldham, and Rochdale, brought the experience he had gained when coaching at Swinton and Blackpool Borough. And, joined by Ray Clarke, another ex-player and amateur Under-19 Rugby League coach, they had that vital asset for a struggling club – a knowledge of the amateur players and the young professionals who had not made the grade with the top clubs. With an upper limit of £2000 placed on any signing, these are the players the coaches have to find. They scour the amateur clubs, both League and Union, always hoping to uncover a future star. In Paul Tomlinson's words, 'The board expect the coaching staff to keep their eyes open for solid professionals, not mercenaries, who will set a good example. They must hope to build a professional framework from a modest situation.' Many are still attracted to the club, with the younger lads being given a two- or three-year contract and the older professionals a one-year contract.

Youngsters like Ian Ince, from the Wigan St Patrick's amateur club; Carmel Sealey, from Waterhead; and Neil Mattison, from Redhill, each received a signing-on fee of £500 and were offered incentive payments over a period of eighteen months. With playing terms of £75 for a win and £25 for a defeat they can hope to earn around £1500 for their season's work. Others, like the Tupaea brothers, Shane and Ashley, from New Zealand, do earn more but, despite promotional work in the ever expanding amateur leagues in the Midlands, and coaching with schools, they will hardly ever earn more than the lowest paid youngster at a top first division club. Yet, despite limited earnings, the club have requests every week for trials from amateurs, and such is the club spirit and the friendships between players, directors and the coaching staff that, as David Parker explains, the players often sign for the strangest of reasons.

'When I went to sign Keith Whiteman, I said to his wife, Julie, that there was a lovely smell coming from the kitchen and was told that it was Keith's favourite rhubarb tart. I immediately went to my father's garden, stripped it of every rhubarb stick and returned with them for Julie to make Keith a few pies. Julie told Keith, "Sign for Mansfield, they are genuine men".'

Though Mansfield are working hard to help local development by trying to field an Under-19 team drawn from east Midlands amateur sides they are at present, owing to costs, restricted to one side with a playing squad of around twenty players. Such are the injuries in a hard contact sport like Rugby League that all manage to get games frequently but a training night in the leafy outskirts of Brighouse, nestling alongside the Pennines, was a much quieter affair than at Central Park. Watched by a curious local resident out walking his dog, Jim Crellin and Ray Clarke put the players through a harsh physical session on the all-weather track at the school fields. With all the Mansfield players northern based, at the moment, such a training area close to the M62 is ideal for those travelling from Lancashire and Yorkshire two evenings a week. But, with travel expenses for training now amounting to £80 a session, Paul Tomlinson, the chairman, admits that the club can only afford two training nights. Despite such limitations and despite the fact that both coaches and players had rushed many miles straight from work, there is a surge of enthusiasm from all at 7 p.m. on Tuesday and Friday evenings. With barely four hours a week in which to prepare a side, most players dashing back home at about 9 p.m. to change out of their work clothes, have tea, and relax, the sessions are naturally pretty concentrated.

Tuesday evening is given over to physical work on the track with the players indulging in sustained interval running, timed sprints and often a series of staggered competitive 200-metre timed races. All the players' times were recorded and each was urged by Jim Crellin to better his times. Brian Handy, a part-time physiotherapist and a former soccer player with Halifax Town, flitted round the track seeing to the odd strain and acting as starter or marker. The players, wearing spikes provided by the club, though in a motley collection of their own jerseys and tracksuits, accept the chiding of Jim Crellin and approach the training in a most serious and disciplined manner. A session in the school sports hall, where each player has his own personal circuit training schedule, sent them tired but happy into the showers, thankful for a rest before Friday's session.

Though that session is not as physically demanding, being a period of conditioning exercises followed by ball work and team training on the school rugby pitch, Jim Crellin demands much more from his players. 'They train voluntarily from 1 June without expenses until mid-July, when we do most of the hard physical work. The majority do weight circuits at home or in a local gymnasium and they go for road runs. We monitor their fitness and the lads know it.' It is obvious that planning and a considerable effort go into the weekly sessions by the coaches, and the players respond well to their demands. But, because of the limitations on the club, Jim Crellin's horizons ultimately have to be limited too. His plan of 'getting out of the bottom six in the second division and approaching mid-table over the next two years' proved a realistic approach as, after only fifteen months in charge, Mansfield Marksman finished seventh in the second division, the highest position in the club's short history, and took part in the end-of-season premiership final play-offs.

Sadly, that success and a thirst for even more, from an ambitious coach, proved Jim Crellin's undoing at Mansfield and highlighted the fine distinction between success and the possibility of extinction for a club new to Rugby League. Though wearied by the constant travel across the Pennines, Crellin would have been prepared to continue with his coaching duties at Mansfield throughout the 1988–89 season and to fulfil his ambition of taking the club into the top four places of the second division. Believing that that could be done only by strengthening his team squad with some better quality players, Crellin insisted that an outlay of £30,000 would be needed for him to spend in the transfer market. Sadly, the board felt unable to sanction such an outlay in view of their impending move to Sutton Town and, as a consequence, their inability to assess future income with any accuracy. Ambitious, and in demand elsewhere for his coaching abilities, it was only natural that Jim Crellin should resign but David Parker's attitude to Crellin's resignation lays bare the realities of life on the lower rungs of Rugby League's ladder.

'Good housekeeping is the most important factor in keeping a club like Mansfield alive. Though we had an excellent coach, who did a first-class job, we dare not spend beyond our means. We might have finished top but been declared insolvent in the process.' Mansfield are still solvent but two more coaches, Billy Platt and Steve Nash, have since left, both unable to carry out their responsibilities with an under-strength squad.

The dream of beating Wigan, offered me by one of Mansfield's young signings, as he contentedly munched his pie and sandwiches in the changing-room after training, is impossible in present circumstances. Despite all his efforts and the efforts of other young members like him, and all the effort and enthusiasm of the directors and coaching staff, we must ask ourselves if all this energy would not be better channelled by a radically new approach to the League's divisional structure. Paul Tomlinson and David Parker, the saviours of Mansfield, certainly think so.

Complaints have frequently been raised in League circles that the mighty, by virtue of the levies taken from their gate receipts, have always shouldered a heavy burden in supporting the weak. The ability of all thirty-four clubs, regardless of their playing strength or financial position, to voice their opinion in the Rugby League's ruling council, prior to the appointment of the new six-man management committee in August 1988, has been cited as a case of the weak leading the strong. Yet, if the code is to advance well beyond the year 2000 and remain in good health, it is just that philanthropic and democratic spirit which must endure to devise a structure catering for both a Wigan and a Mansfield under the same roof, perhaps not with equal rights, but certainly with equal opportunities.

In my view, the new structure should be a pyramid with, at the apex, premier clubs, possibly with full-time professional players. In the middle, and a very solid middle too, should be a core of part-time professional teams, strengthened and fostered from a large base of amateurs. That large base is necessary to renew the talent in the professional leagues, provide enjoyment for thousands of

Rugby League adherents, and cultivate a large spectator interest nationally. The base of the pyramid is well on the way to being achieved and already Rugby League, like the Heineken advertisements, 'has touched the parts that other sports haven't reached'. But to build the two upper layers of the pyramid the league structure demands revision. In a sport which, quite rightly, encourages Mansfield Marksman and others like them to run onto the same field as the mighty Wigan there must be a system which allows each club to find its level nationally, give it time and the resources to gather its finances and its playing strength, and then give that club a real opportunity to move forward. I believe a re-vamped three-division structure would achieve this.

At present all thirty-four professional clubs are placed in two divisions with rugby ability being the only criterion for entrance to the first division or to joining the twenty clubs in the second division. Owing to the large number of clubs in the lower division and the inordinately large amount of cup competitions in which all the clubs take part, one of the great weaknesses of the second division is that not all the clubs play each other but only a section of the clubs on a yearly rota basis. In theory, and often in practice, the champions can be installed at the end of the season without having played the strength of the teams below them. This is not a satisfactory state of affairs and does not offer equal opportunities to the clubs. I would strongly urge the adoption of a three-division system which would offer greater incentives to players and their coaches, raise the image of the League code at the highest levels, provide true competition for all, and help to increase even further the rise in attendances over the past couple of seasons.

The first division would consist of twelve teams, two less than the present number, allowing for a second and third division of eleven teams each, though I would add that, because of the greater flexibility within my proposed third division, these numbers could be easily increased over the next few years. The giants Wigan, Widnes, Leeds, St Helens, Hull, Salford and so on – with large conurbations from which to draw spectators, modern stadiums, and good amateur and schoolboy feeder systems – would obviously, as today, provide the bulk of the first division. Because the top contracted players can now earn such good money, and because of the continuing incidence of unemployment in the north, many contemporary players, perhaps not by choice, have already established themselves as full-time professionals.

This arrangement should continue if an individual club wanted it to. A second division of eleven clubs would contain some of the teams in the heartland of Rugby League: if Leigh, Oldham, Wakefield Trinity, Barrow, and Featherstone, all of whom have endured spells in the second division recently, were to make up a division alongside new and re-emerging clubs such as Sheffield Eagles, Whitehaven and Doncaster, then we would have a strong and well supported competition. Gates, I am sure, would increase as battles for promotion and relegation caught the fans' attention. The players would all be, as now, part-time professionals and would no doubt be made up of young aspirants, experienced former first division stars, and a sprinkling of overseas talent. In my view that is the right combination for success, at not too great a cost.

A third division would thus contain many of those clubs, like Batley or Huddersfield, who can point to many glorious years of Rugby League history but who have sadly fallen upon harder times. Such clubs in a smaller and less intense competition could find time to regroup their finances and foster the supply of local amateur talent in their areas. New clubs like Fulham, Carlisle, and Mansfield Marksman themselves could ease their way into Rugby League, pick up those vital wins needed to cultivate team spirit, and give encouragement to spectators in these all important early years. By not meeting the stronger sides, save in cup ties, such clubs would have a better chance to develop local amateur talent and encourage junior Rugby Union signings who may have little or no experience of the game.

There would be no need for the new clubs in new areas to face the huge expense of importing the old northern professionals for short-term service. All players in the third division need not be professionals; a club, if finances were strained, could operate with three or four paid players alongside amateurs, who, as in major Union clubs, could be paid liberal expenses until they had proved their worth for contracts. The playing staff and the financial commitments could be flexible. If the clubs which now languish in thirteenth to sixteenth positions in the present second division and which, after every December, have little to play for, were to be seen battling for promotion from the third division, then the crowd appeal must be greater. Gates at the bottom clubs could not be less than they are now, though I do not think that problem need occupy too much of the league management committee's time. Provided a club is financially viable and has correctly costed its expenditure on players, it is not only valuable as a nursery for talent, but also adds to the national identity of Rugby League. The increased sponsorship attracted to central funds by the creation of a truly national sport and the gate levies from the élite clubs would continue to help survival.

A last thought: all new clubs joining the Rugby League in future must be given time to put down roots in their area and cultivate their own spectator interest. Of the six new clubs to join the Rugby Football League in the 1980s – Fulham, Carlisle, Mansfield, Sheffield Eagles, Kent Invicta and Cardiff – it is significant that the two who failed to stay the course, Kent Invicta and Cardiff, were seriously undercapitalised but neither had, nor were given, sufficient time to develop any natural roots. In common with the other four clubs, Mansfield Marksman have appointed two directors, Cec Thompson and Alastair Auld, to liaise with representatives of amateur teams in Derbyshire and Nottinghamshire, forming an umbrella organisation for the development of Rugby League in those counties. Curtain raisers involving area teams, such as Garibaldi and Clowne, are held at the ground and already upwards of a dozen schools have tasted Rugby League when eighteen months ago none had done so.

I have no doubts that the upper body of the pyramid structure which I envisage would be financially strong enough and, in terms of playing strength, powerful enough to enhance further the code's reputation with spectacular matches. But its support and strength would need to lie in the endeavours of those second and third division teams which, in turn, would be supported by and be supportive of the largest section at the base. That base, the British Amateur Rugby League, has witnessed phenomenal growth over the past fifteen years and, thankfully, looks set for even further expansion.

7

A National Identity

The strides made in recent years by the British Amateur Rugby League Association (BARLA) have been truly staggering in relation to other sporting bodies. Formed in 1973, at a time when amateur Rugby League was in its death throes, and with a bank balance of only £25, the governing body has presided over an increase of 1000 teams and 25,000 players throughout the country in those sixteen years. They have seen their amateur representative sides at all levels, youth and open age, tour Papua New Guinea, Australia, and New Zealand and have welcomed similar parties from overseas to British shores.

Perhaps the most important development nationally in this last decade and a half has been the appointment of regional development officers, especially of Tom O'Donovan as BARLA's national development officer in April 1988. These regional officers, under O'Donovan's guidance, are now encouraging workers on League's behalf at grassroots level; already in areas such as Warrington, Wigan, Sheffield and Calderdale, where development officer appointments have been made in conjunction with local councils, renewed interest in Rugby League is there for all to see. Their influence in the south, Midlands, and north-east, where the expertise of such area organisers as David Kay, Ken Johnson, and Bev Risman is adding to the hard work done in the past by countless pioneers and devotees of Rugby League, is now reaping huge rewards for the League code. BARLA proudly boasts that its aim is to have a League side in every major city and town in England by 1995, the centenary of the Rugby Football League, and it really does appear that Maurice Oldroyd, the national administrator, and his men are well on their way to achieving that goal.

The National Amateur League and, as from September 1989, its newly formed second division, will continue to be BARLA's flagship. Since its introduction in 1986 the National Amateur League, containing ten of the major northern sides, such as Pilkington Recs, Milford, Millom, West Hull, and Wigan St Patrick's, has attracted considerable media coverage and sponsorship while the standard and presentation of the rugby has been of the highest quality. All the clubs, especially the new entrants at second division level, have been carefully vetted as to their playing strength, their administrative capabilities and ground and club house facilities. Hopefully, if expansion continues at the rate it has for the past decade then we may see clubs entering the National League via its second division from much further afield than traditional Rugby League playing areas. Standards may vary, as they do in Union, in different parts of the country, but there is no doubting the BARLA clubs' enthusiasm, commitment, and industry. And that enthusiasm must be rewarded further by the creation in the 1990s of perhaps another two divisions from the south.

In London, Rugby League is looking healthier than at any previous time with the older clubs, South London Wanderers, London Colonials, Hemel Hempstead and so on now being pressed by Hornsey Lambs, Cambridge City, and Essex Scimitars. Further success in the capital is surely assured now that a development officer, Ken Johnson, has been appointed for the London region. Ken, an ex-teacher and one of the driving forces behind Hornsey Lambs, will be directly responsible to the national development officer, Tom O'Donovan. The code now prospers in the Midlands, and the south-west, and maintains a foothold in Wales; strong sides at Aberavon, Gloucester, Bristol, Bath, Redditch, and Wolverhampton are setting the pace. In Nottinghamshire, Derbyshire and surrounding areas a league of eleven teams, from such areas as Leicester, Nottingham, Clowne, and Garibaldi maintain the surge in interest. And in the north-east, at Durham, Hartlepool and Newcastle, the 13-a-side code is thriving. Even the Civil Service, usually the most conservative of bodies, has introduced an annual competition between its regional departments. Moves are afoot to introduce Rugby League to the armed services. In the days of national service many great Rugby League players, such as Alex Murphy, Jim Challinor, Mick Sullivan, Phil Jackson and Billy Boston were forced to play Rugby Union for their units. And many, like Boston and Jackson, helped to elevate some of those units, such as the Royal Signals at Catterick in the 1950s, onto the nation's sports pages by their deeds in the 15-a-side code.

Developments in the north, where sparkling new clubhouses have mushroomed and new team names at all age-levels have appeared in the ever-increasing leagues, have possibly exceeded all expectations; there are now over 100 clubs in the North-west Lancashire League alone. Many of the fixtures, even when compared to the professional game, are now so attractive and so well supported that a crowd of 4333 and receipts of over £4000 were recorded at a recent St Annes v. Saddleworth Rangers match in the Oldham district. The amateur game can only grow from strength to strength, and nourish even more the professional side of the code now that long standing problems between the professional clubs' Colts rugby and BARLA's youth teams have been satisfactorily resolved.

Sadly, the wrangling between the professional body and BARLA over Colts rugby caused considerable friction, and relationships between the two governing bodies were soured by lack of agreement over the development of Under-19 players. Many within the professional game saw the fielding of Under-19 Colts teams at clubs like Leeds, Wigan, St Helens and Hull, in a two division structure, as a high-grade nursery of talent for the professional clubs themselves. Many of the players were already young professionals, signed by the club at 17 years of age, and playing alongside amateurs in the same team. Opponents of the Colts leagues stressed that all youth rugby should come under the jurisdiction of BARLA and argued that the promotion of Colts rugby was counterproductive to the amateur aims. Many insisted that the presence of a Colts team in a town denuded the local amateur clubs of their best players and robbed many youngsters of their chance of youth international amateur honours. Whatever the arguments, the lack of a common approach was not good for the game.

Thankfully, after much painstaking work on the part of the Rugby Football League, BARLA, and the Sports Council the matter was at last resolved in April 1988. Development areas were established, with each professional club acting as an umbrella for the amateur clubs in its geographical catchment area and being given first option on signing amateur players from its area. In return, the professional clubs must assist with coaching at Under-19 level and so help prepare teams for the Under-19 midweek league, involving representative sides based on these designated catchment areas. These arrangements, now agreed upon, have brought all youth rugby effectively under the control of BARLA and, with backing from the Rugby League Foundation, there is no reason why the game at youth level should not prosper. The

Rugby League Foundation, a charitable body consisting of ten representatives from the professional, amateur, and schools sections, had been formed in 1987 to encourage and finance the development of the game, particularly at school and youth levels. An indication of its importance to youth rugby can be seen in its injection of £100,000 into the development of the amateur game in its first year and, with the recruitment of financial backers like British Coal, it is possible that a great deal more money will be invested in the game over the next year or two.

Indeed, the midweek Under-19 league, now sponsored by British Coal in a £120,000 deal spread over three years, has been a huge success, with leading sides like St Helens, Castleford and Hull attracting good crowds. Of most value has been the creation of Under-19 sides in hitherto virgin territory in London, South Yorkshire, and the Midlands. Richard Blackman (Oldham), Carl Cooper (St Helens), Mike Dixon (Hull), and Neil Flanagan (Oldham) are typical of promising youngsters who are serving their apprenticeship in this highly competitive league.

The opening of BARLA's first centre of excellence in December 1988, made possible by a grant of £188,000 from the former Greater Manchester Council, will be immensely helpful in moulding such young stars. The floodlit six-acre site at Leigh has two playing areas, a small pitch for mini-rugby and a purpose built multi-gym. Such excellent facilities, supervised by another development officer, Dennis McHugh, is available for all – from the youngest schoolboys to the Great Britain international team.

Throughout the 1980s BARLA emerged with great success from confrontations with the Rugby Football Union and with its own professional body in Rugby League. Now the governing body must devote its energies to achieving a national identity for the game. The sudden spurt in the last few years to gain that goal has been mirrored in the battles, achievements, and frustrations of a club like Cheltenham, who now represent the ever widening base of Rugby League's ideal pyramid structure. RL clubs at Cheltenham, Gloucester, Bath, and Leicester can, from humble beginnings, if the will and playing strength is there, achieve professional status. A dream? Possibly. But a dream no more unrealistic than that facing Lionel Hurst, Cheltenham's founder, back in September 1984.

Though the myth that amateur League teams in the south of England are populated by ageing exiled northerners reliving the game of their youth is a misconception there is no denying the truth that most clubs are founded by a northerner. And Lionel Hurst, a small, softly spoken advocate in criminal law, is no exception. Taken to Warrington as a youngster in the early 1960s by his father, the club doctor of the previous decade, Lionel developed a passion for the League code which, despite playing alongside Bill Beaumont, the former England RU captain when both were at Ellesmere College, never deserted him, even when he left for the south. That departure ran parallel with a similar movement from Wirral in Cheshire by Craig Furlong, an ex-Rugby Union player, and a founder member, with Lionel Hurst, of the Cheltenham club. From an advertisement in the *Gloucestershire Echo*, announcing a Rugby League appreciation society and training sessions at the Cheltenham YMCA, a total of eight players were attracted for that first training session, boosted by the appearance of a dozen lads from the Aberavon League club which acted as a great morale lifter to Lionel. In any event Craig Furlong and Lionel Hurst were on the move and, with persuasion, enough bodies were assembled on 7 October 1984 to play the first Rugby League match in Cheltenham since the staging of an exhibition Test match between Great Britain and Australia back in 1908. Another historic event was about to take place; but not before Lionel Hurst, while on the way to the ground in his car, had picked up a hitch-hiker, and, before offering the lift, had gained a promise from him that he would play in this inaugural game. He duly scored a try in Cheltenham's 14-56 defeat by a Welsh President's XIII.

Exiled northerners quickly appeared on the scene once a match had taken place but there was also no real shortage of Rugby Union players willing to have a go at the new code. Indeed such was the fear and animosity from the local Union fraternity that the Cheltenham Rugby Union club refused to allow the new League club to use the council-owned stadium when it was not in use by themselves. Cheltenham Civil Service, on hearing that members were playing for the Cheltenham ARLFC, absurdly tried to ban their members from doing so by placing notices to that effect at their place of work.

'We lost many quality players during this period who had joined us from the junior Rugby Union clubs. The clubs were afraid. They did not believe there was such a thing as amateur Rugby League. They thought we were all professionals,' declares Lionel. But the breakthrough had been achieved, the Cheltenham club acted as the catalyst for the formation of a South-west League with teams from Gloucester, Bristol, Redditch, Bath and Plymouth joining in, and, eventually, even £500 of sponsorship money was provided by a local wine bar.

Indeed, once clear of the initial anti-League controversy, the League club has now become, in the words of Craig Furlong, still a playing member, 'accepted as part of the Cheltenham scene. We receive good press coverage, have a sympathetic public, and are rapidly breaking down misguided beliefs traditionally held about Rugby League.' Ironically, the club now shares its ground with a local Rugby Union club, Cheltenham North, but such has been the development within the space of only four years that already Lionel Hurst has launched into yet another gamble, a bold one, but one which could produce even more dramatic results for Rugby League if successful in Cheltenham.

In an attempt to cut travel costs and to convert more players to the game, as an experiment for the 1987–88 Season, the Cheltenham club, technically, dissolved. Its players scattered round Cheltenham with the intention of each forming groups of players who would in turn take part in a six-team 9-a-side Cheltenham & District Rugby league competition. Such an arrangement, it was hoped, would generate greater enthusiasm for the League code within Cheltenham. Lionel Hurst saw this as the next stage of development in the production of players and a League identity in the area.

Though the experiment was not a total success, since the name of Cheltenham disappeared from the south-west Rugby League scene, it did, in Hurst's words, 'generate many new players for the following season when we reformed as Cheltenham and the experiment did get more new lads playing Rugby League.' That influx of new playing members allowed Cheltenham to take the honours at the Chester Sevens, a tournament specifically designed for emerging clubs, in August 1988, and such was the fervour of League during the 1987–88 season, that Cheltenham has been able to maintain the town team alongside their mini-league. Indeed, such has been their impact that a nationally known insurance company, Endsleigh, is now their major sponsor. That is a far cry from help from a local wine bar in the club's early days.

Lionel Hurst, Craig Furlong, David Kay, the south-west's development officer, and others like them are enjoying their involvement within amateur Rugby League. The professional game, through television, will present the sport to countless millions still having little connection with or knowledge of it. But it is clubs like Cheltenham, Thatto Heath, and Millom amateur Rugby League clubs which provide the bulk of the game's players. Rugby League's base is now a solid one and growing stronger every season; yet, whatever standard of team, and whether amateur or professional, that spectators watch, it is the duty of all to produce a standard of excellence at the top. The interest in League that sprang immediately from Great Britain's magnificent third Test win over Australia in the summer of 1988 resulted in record advance season ticket sales at clubs like Widnes and St Helens. Those high standards of skill and commitment, absent from British Rugby League for so long, have resurfaced with players of a standard similar to those great players I watched as a youngster or played with as a young man. There is no doubt that, in turn, the same high standards will brush off onto the amateur game.

8

Great Days, Memorable Players

Any young lad living in the northern towns of Warrington, Oldham, or Wakefield in the immediate post-war years, and attracted to Rugby League, might have had few material possessions but he could be cocooned in a world of dreams and fantasies. I was no exception. My dreams and fantasies came from a regular diet of Saturday afternoon Rugby League at the Knowsley Road home of St Helens RLFC. Wrapped in a red and white scarf, clutching a large wooden rattle (now, sadly, no longer seen) and wearing my compulsory school cap, I was usually to be found with my head between the decrepit wooden railings which surrounded the pitch. That wooden railing, despite its lean to an angle of 40° at the Kop end, was the perfect vantage point for being the first on the ground to see the teams coming out of the players' tunnel and on to the field. That vantage point, though, had to be gained by queuing for entrance to the ground for over two hours before the kick-off, followed by a mad dash from the turnstiles at one corner of the ground in an effort to beat the other kids racing from the turnstiles at the other corner of the Kop.

The matches seemed to take place in the distance, like an old feature film flickering intermittently before one's eyes, for the first forty minutes of the game was usually spent in arguments over the right to sit on top of the fence and in consuming large quantities of sweets, crisps, and pop. Whether driven away by the poor quality of the play or the regularity of St Helens's defeats in those days, the second half consisted of a game of touch rugby on the rubble-strewn clearing behind the Kop with my cap, rolled up and held firm with an elastic band, as the ball. The final score of the Saints match was easily observed on the faces of the spectators who picked their unsteady way down the banking at the back of the Kop, then studded with bricks, concrete slabs, and sprouting brambles. Amid mutterings of 'What a pack of forwards, no wonder they're called the "easy six",' we left for home, seeking refuge from the dark, only to curl round the radio to await the crackling tones of Alan Dixon or Harry Sunderland on Radio North at 6.30 p.m., who reported on yet more heroes of my Rugby League world. One minute I would be Clive Churchill, the diminutive but fearless Australian full-back, or Ernest Ward, the most majestic of Great Britain centres, or big Frank Whitcombe, the Bradford Northern steamroller prop – heroes all to a young lad, just as, no doubt, the names of Joe Lydon, Wally Lewis, and Ellery Hanley are today.

Many of my contemporaries of forty years ago still lean on the new concrete wall at Knowsley Road, all still worshipping at the feet of their heroes, yet still locked in their minds will be the memories of players of our school-days, and players of my playing days. Unlike the spectators on the terraces or in the stands, I have had the good fortune to observe the players of the past forty or so years both subjectively and objectively as spectator, player, and commentator. As I have explained, their playing roles may have changed and my appreciation of the players may have altered from one of naive adulation to one of critical analysis but my estimation of their abilities has never wavered; indeed those of the past have possibly increased in worth. The cry of 'They're not as good as they were in my day' must be treated always with considerable caution and the comments of 'Your team would have murdered this present-day outfit' must be put in perspective. Such comments are often good for the ego but replies in the affirmative must be treated with caution.

If there is truth in Graham Lowe's belief that 'talent is God-given', then talent must always be unchanging and unending, whatever the changed circumstances of Rugby League. Playing styles have changed, physical shapes, especially in the pack, have altered, the laws have been rewritten, and even the points scoring system has not escaped an overhaul, yet talented players of forty years ago must at least be the equals of our present-day players. Despite my great pride in my personal fitness when playing in the 1960s I would even be happy to concede that standards of fitness and mental preparation for a game are now superior to those of previous eras.

Yet I'm not so certain whether I accept the view that the modern player has advanced in skills beyond the standards set by the players of the 1950s. The issue must be a personal one, culled from one's own vivid memories. My memories of standing in a 30,000 crowd at Fartown, Huddersfield in 1952 and being thrilled at the sight of Lionel Cooper, their giant wing, thundering for the try-line are as distinct today as the sight of Wigan's Henderson Gill using every ounce of muscle to outpace the Hull full-back, Gary Kemble, in that never-to-be-forgotten Challenge Cup final of 1985. The grace and finesse of Tom Van Vollenhoven, the St Helens Springbok wing, as he sped along the touchline was a sight to behold in my playing days. The talents of all three were truly 'God-given' but can one measure such talents alongside the talents of another era? I would say the answer is 'yes', but it must be an answer fraught with argument and the conclusion can only be a subjective one.

I can easily select three teams of British players from the three periods with which I have been associated, but each one would be selected from a different standpoint. My dream team for the period between 1946–61 naturally consists of players observed from beyond the wooden railing and so entertainment value must be the main criterion. A team from my playing days with St Helens and Widnes between 1961–72 would be selected on a more professional basis as being the ideal combination to achieve a win, while a team of the 1980s, a period in which I have watched Rugby League as a commentator, would be viewed from both standpoints. The last team would of course be selected after a greater degree of objective criticism. But whatever the teams I have chosen, I have no doubt that arguments will rage as to the merits of the players and, especially, which would be the best of the three sides were each to play against the others at the peak of their prowess. My ego would like the team from my own playing days to be the victor, though accepted opinion would probably point to the greatness of the early post-war period. But can one argue with the march of physical and technical development shown by the heroes of the 1980s? The reader must make up his own mind.

1946–61. 'The Spectator'

Martin Ryan (Wigan); Frank Castle (Barrow), Ernest Ward (Bradford Northern) (capt.), Douglas Greenall (St Helens), Stan McCormick (St Helens); Willie Horne (Barrow), Gerry Helme (Warrington); Ken Gee (Wigan), Joe Egan (Wigan), Alan Prescott (St Helens), Trevor Foster (Bradford Northern), Ken Traill (Bradford Northern and Halifax), David Valentine (Huddersfield)

Substitutes Ernie Ashcroft (Wigan), Billy Ivison (Workington Town).

1 **Martin Ryan.** A Great Britain tourist in 1946 and 1950, Martin was the attacking full-back *par excellence*. His incursions into the Wigan threequarter line added another dimension to the side's attacking prowess at a time when most full-backs were still of the solid, defensive type, more concerned with stopping tries and kicking upfield than with initiating tries.

2 **Frank Castle.** Castle's signing from Coventry Rugby Union club coincided with Barrow's greatest period of success in the 1950s and it was Frank's deceptive change of pace and body swerve which contributed to that success. Sadly, early injuries on the 1954 tour of Australia reduced his appearances to only five matches on that tour.

3 **Ernest Ward (captain).** Ward's Lance Todd Trophy win as man-of-the-match in Bradford Northern's Challenge Cup win over Halifax in 1949, and his record 34 points in a Great Britain match at Mackay when accompanying the 1946 tourists bears testimony to the abilities of this master tactician. A dream partner for any winger, Ernest was a stylish player, a well balanced runner who timed his passes superbly. Having starred in over twenty Tests his love for Rugby League shone through in his work for the Lions and Bradford Northern past-players associations.

4 **'Douggie' Greenall.** One of the true characters of the game whose appearance on a ground would herald the cry of 'Give 'em "Mammy", Doug'. It was his known fondness for Al Jolson songs that gave rise to his nickname as much as his lethal tackling which saw him fly through the air, arms outstretched, to put his opponents somewhat dubiously 'to sleep'. Feared by the Australians, whose banner headline 'Killer Greenall arrives today' bore testimony to his defence, he was none the less the most crafty of centres. His nursing of the ex-Springbok RU wing, Tom Van Vollenhoven, into Rugby League was masterly.

5 **Stan McCormick**. Known as the 'prince of sidesteppers', Stan loved nothing more than to taunt his opponents with his sidestepping from one side of the field to the other, often scoring on his opposite wing. A professional sprinter in his heyday, he held the world record transfer fee at £4000 in 1948 when he was signed by St Helens from the now defunct club, Belle Vue Rangers. His skills at mastering the art of the interception had few equals. A golden memory of mine will always be the look on the face of the Australian full-back, Clive Churchill, when, about to put his colleague, Noel Pidding, over for a try at St Helens, he saw McCormick snatch the ball and race ninety yards for a try at the other end. Precision timing!

6 **Willie Horne**. This tactical genius rarely looked rugged enough to survive a game of Rugby League yet his delicate skills enabled him to triumph on two Lions tours in 1946 and 1950. A small, wiry man, Willie Horne ghosted through opposition defences and opened up gaps with the timing of his passes. His speciality, the grubber kick or chip kick, also split many a defence. His captaincy at Wembley in Barrow's Challenge Cup final defeat of Workington Town in 1955 was a fitting reward for a man who carried the club to its greatest fortunes.

7 **Gerry Helme**. Helme will always be remembered by men for his tackle, known as the 'Cumberland throw', whereby this tiny scrum-half would seize a giant forward's outstretched hand, thrust out a leg, and send him cartwheeling to the ground. Having seen the 16-stone prop, Alan Prescott, suffer at Gerry's hands I can understand why this tackle is now banned. Yet he was a fiery, dynamic player, displaying dazzling skills, which earned him the distinction of being the only man to win two Lance Todd Trophies as the man-of-the-match in the 1950 and 1954 Challenge Cup finals. Helme's matchwinning try in that never-to-be-

forgotten 1954 Cup final replay against Halifax at Odsal which attracted a world record gate of 102,569 was indicative of his sharp acceleration away from the scrum.

8 **Ken Gee**. Gee was truly a giant of a man at 16-stone and a giant too for over twenty years with Wigan. In the days of matches containing up to fifty scrums, his reputation as a ball winner was awesome, as was his reputation for handling the ball once it had been won. He somehow found the energy to be a successful goalkicker too, a rarity for a prop today, and even topped the kicking charts with 133 goals in 1949–50.

9 **Joe Egan**. Egan surprisingly began his career at Wigan as a full-back, a position in which he probably developed his fine ball-handling skills. Yet as a hooker he reigned supreme between 1937–50 until his surprise world-record transfer at £5000 to the club's near neighbours, Leigh. A great tactical thinker about the game I was especially grateful for his knowledge when playing under him when he was coach at Widnes in the late 1960s.

10 **Alan Prescott**. My first coach in 1961 at St Helens was able to command respect by his deeds on two British tours to Australia in 1954 and 1958. When I complained of a sprung shoulder in a match at Swinton and was promptly told to pack in the scrum on the blind side so that it would hurt less how could I complain to a man who had led his Test side to victory in 1958 with a broken arm? The sight of this powerful red-haired forward charging at speed through the opposition would rouse the terraces.

11 **Trevor Foster**. This ex-Newport RU and Bradford Northern second row was a prolific try scorer, registering over 140 tries in his career. Yet he could almost make the ball talk, such was his skill when it was in his large hands. A tireless worker, Foster played in all three of Bradford's Cup final appearances between 1947–49, and was proud

to represent the Welsh Services RU during the war when the League and Union fraternity joined forces.

12 **Ken Traill.** Traill was a strong tackling forward who saw service with both Bradford and Halifax and who perfected the art of ball distribution to his colleagues in support. He was a ferocious tackler, which stood him in good stead on the Australian tours of 1950 and 1954.

13 **David Valentine.** This craggy Scot from Hawick RU and Huddersfield RL was an inspirational loose forward who skippered a team of 'no hopers' to Great Britain's first World Cup success in 1954. A hard man, who led by example, his appetite for hard work earned David fifteen Test caps between 1948–54.

14 **Ernie Ashcroft.** This classy centre won many championship and cup honours with Wigan in the immediate post-war years, his best performance possibly being his two match-winning tries against Huddersfield in the 1946 Championship final at Manchester City's Maine Road ground. He was a truly elegant footballer.

15 **Billy Ivison.** Ivison was awarded the Lance Todd Trophy in Workington Town's only Challenge Cup win over Featherstone Rovers in 1952. Never capped for Great Britain, yet in my opinion the equal of all his contemporaries. Only 5 foot 10 inches in height he was a hard Cumbrian forward, uncompromising in defence and with a shrewd eye for an opening on attack. Being so low to the ground Ivison was a very difficult man to stop.

The years from 1946 to 1961 saw few major law changes in Rugby League as both spectators and administrators enjoyed a period of large crowds and quality players. What law changes were introduced were mostly cosmetic and did not effect any change in the nature and style of play. As before the war, the emphasis on forward play and a reliance on solid scrummaging was still paramount and the side I have selected reflects that priority. In matches which averaged upwards of sixty scrums, a specialist hooker was usually the first man selected in all teams, invariably accompanied by two large durable props, able to withstand the rigours of both scrummaging and loose play. A front row of Gee, Egan, and Prescott would be more than equal to that task. The unlimited-tackle law, whereby a team in possession could retain the ball until it committed an offence, was of course in operation throughout this fifteen-year period with the result that there was greater concentration on forward play in midfield. Though forwards like Trevor Foster could show a fine turn of speed and score tries regularly, the overall pace of the pack was slower while the size of the pack was bigger. Most packs included a couple of skilled, constructive ball players, as I have done in the inclusion of Joe Egan and Dave Valentine, who sent the forwards driving down the middle of the pitch with short interpassing. This war of attrition, though not very spectacular, was still enjoyed by the huge crowds whose 'oohs' and 'aahs' bore testimony to their delight in physical confrontation.

Scrum-halves played much closer to the pack than their modern counterparts, though I must admit that Andy Gregory, the current Great Britain no. 7, plays a similar role to Gerry Helme forty years ago. Helme would be snapping at the heels of his forwards, working in concert with his loose forward, who was able to break early from the scrum in those days, and was always ready to throw the ball out wide. Though defences were much stronger and the tackling more effective than we have become accustomed to in Britain in the 1980s, one of the ironies of the style of play in the 1940s and 1950s was that there was far more room down the flanks for wingers and constructive centres. The bigger, heavier forwards were often too tired to stray out towards the touchlines and, after performing fifty or sixty tackles they rarely had the breath to cover across the pitch in the last twenty minutes. Hence those two decades were the eras of great wingers and it is significant that many of our club try-scoring records were achieved at that time, by fast running wingmen, often from overseas. Brian Bevan (Warrington), Tom Van Vollenhoven (St Helens), and Jack McLean (Bradford Northern) readily spring to mind.

In my selected team Frank Castle and Stan McCormick were two fast and elusive wingers who were only too pleased to take advantage of such scoring opportunities carved out by constructive centres and by the full-back Martin Ryan. The immediate post-war era was also to see a change in full-back play with the days of the purely goal-kicking, defensive-minded full-back on the wane and with an exciting runner like Wigan's Martin Ryan heralding the age of the attacking full-back. Many full-backs were still necessary for goal-kicks; there was then no differential penalty at scrum offences and so few sides went into battle without a specialist goal-kicker, such were the number of shots afforded him. Ernest Ward or Willie Horne would have taken care of this aspect of play. The side selected would certainly be a powerful one and one which I would have liked to have seen playing against a team picked from my contemporaries of the 1960s and early 1970s. The issue, I think, would have been a close one.

1961–72. 'The Player'

Ken Gowers (Swinton); Billy Boston (Wigan), Eric Ashton (Wigan), Neil Fox (Wakefield Trinity), Mick Sullivan (Huddersfield, Wigan, St Helens); Alan Hardisty (Castleford), Alex Murphy (St Helens, Leigh, Warrington); Brian McTigue (Wigan), Johnny Ward (Castleford), Cliff Watson (St Helens), Derek Turner (Oldham, Wakefield

Trinity), Dick Huddart (Whitehaven, St Helens), Vince Karalius (St Helens, Widnes)

Substitutes Roger Millward (Castleford, Hull KR), John Whiteley (Hull).

1 **Ken Gowers.** Though I was only occasionally on the receiving end of the brilliant Swinton attacking machine in the early 1960s I always admired the positional play, speed off the mark, and eye for an opening of Ken at full-back. His thrusts upfield and switches of play in midfield, as Swinton worked their series of back moves, were invariably performed with perfect precision. His fourteen Test caps in the 1960s were well deserved. Nor was he lacking in goal-kicking skills either, having kicked a club record of 12 goals in a match against Liverpool City.

2 **Billy Boston.** I am sure I still feel pain in my shoulders from those attempted tackles of twenty years ago! Selected for the Great Britain tour of 1954 to Australia after only five appearances for Wigan, the Cardiff RU wing repaid the selectors' confidence by scoring 36 tries on the tour. His phenomenal pace and swerve, his strength, hand-off and bouncing bulk had defenders in fear of him. Bruised and battered bodies frequently littered the pitch after one of his touchline dashes. His ability to play at centre or stand-off indicates Billy's all-round rugby skills and his perfection of the crash tackle on the opposite centre is an art rarely practised these days.

3 **Eric Ashton (captain).** Eric shades Alan Davies (Oldham) in my selection because of his uncanny understanding and partnership with Boston when they were together at Wigan. Their scissors or dummy scissors moves were timed to perfection. Eric captained Wigan on six Wembley appearances and led the British tourists to Australia in 1962. A tall player of over 6 foot, Ashton was always able to pass

the ball out of the tackle and was rarely grounded without doing something constructive with the ball.

4 **Neil Fox.** This huge 15-stone centre could drive his bulk at speed through the tightest of defences and, amazingly for such a big man, could also display the neatest of ball handling skills. Sadly, injury robbed him of a place on the 1968 World Cup tour, of which I was a member: his solid presence in midfield was missed. Being one of an elite band of players who continued to play Rugby League at forty years of age his career lasted from 1955 to 1979, and he amassed a world record number of 6220 points.

5 **Mick Sullivan.** Sullivan's record number of Great Britain appearances (forty-six) and his record number of Test tries (forty) indicate Mick's abilities as a strong running, hard tackling wing. He was a fiery character and always a colourful team-mate of mine whose physical clashes with the Australian Test winger Peter Dimond at times deserved an X certificate. He was another strong exponent of the art of the winger moving inside to crash tackle the opposite centre.

6 **Alan Hardisty.** Alan was a Test player who often seemed to go missing in a match and then strike with deadly accuracy for a try or an interception when the opposition was least prepared. A wiry, nimble half-back, Alan had blistering acceleration allied to a sharp rugby brain.

7 **Alex Murphy.** Murphy was the boy prodigy, signed on his sixteenth birthday for £80; in my opinion he was without equal in his era. He possessed every skill imaginable for the scrum-half position – quick thinking, confidence, strength, rugby acumen and above all speed. Alex's incredible pace off the mark served him well in twenty-seven Test appearances and four Challenge Cup-winning appearances at Wembley but rarely better than in one Lancashire

Cup match against Swinton in which I was playing. He put the ball in the scrum, picked it up from beneath my feet at the back and placed it between the posts twenty-five yards away before I had removed my head from the scrum. A genius!

8 **Brian McTigue.** Brian started his career like Joe Egan, as a full-back with Wigan, but became one of the finest ever ball distributors in the forward style of the unlimited tackle days. Paul Daniels, the magician, would have wondered at Brian's sleight of hand with a ball. His tackling was fierce and my chin can testify to his considerable abilities as a boxer in his youth.

9 **Johnny Ward.** This short stocky Castleford hooker, though not at the top of his profession for too long, was a good ball winner in the scrum and above all a shrewd and skilful tactician. His distribution to his pack colleagues was rarely found wanting and he perfected the dummy and defence splitting run at the play-the-ball to good effect. Four Test caps were no true reward for his talents.

10 **Cliff Watson.** Cliff, an ex-Dudley Kingswinford RU player, who replied to a St Helens newspaper advertisement requesting players, was the strongest man I ever played with. Though lacking an index finger on one hand he had few handling problems, delighting in taking the ball directly up to the opposition in fierce bull-like charges. His tackling, in which he usually enveloped his opponent like a spider pouncing on a fly, was awesome to behold. Highly respected by the Australians from his tours to that country, he guested with the Sydney side Cronulla for a short period in the early 1970s.

11 **Derek Turner.** Nicknamed 'Rocky' for obvious reasons, such was his toughness in the tackle, Derek usually played at loose forward. He was a thinker about the game yet his

rugged approach put fire into the rest of the pack whenever he played. His twenty-four Test caps were earned in both the no. 11 and no. 13 positions.

12 **Dick Huddart.** I had the pleasure of playing alongside this speedy, strong running Cumbrian forward, whose forte was to break tackles and streak thirty or forty yards to the try-line. His powerful hand-off and hip sway fended off many an opponent both here and in Australia where he played with distinction for the St George club in Sydney.

13 **Vince Karalius.** Vince's deeds on the 1958 tour of Australia, where he scattered Aussie forwards around the pitch like confetti, his strong surging runs earning him the nickname of the 'Wild Bull of the Pampas', are legendary. He was an inspirational player who helped both St Helens and Widnes to Challenge Cup triumphs. His technique of holding the ball almost chest high well away from the body allowed him to pass the ball frequently out of the tackle to either side. As a no. 13 he perfected all the skills around the scrum which, as I have indicated, are now sadly lacking in the modern game.

14 **Roger Millward.** 'Roger the Dodger' fulfilled all the promise he had shown as a sixteen-year-old schoolboy when featured in a series of youth matches on Sunday afternoons on ITV in the early 1960s. With five trips to Australia, twenty-eight Test appearances, and with a Test career spanning almost thirteen years Roger was something special. Though only 5 foot 4 inches in height and weighing 10 stone 10 lb. he had a nimble brain, equally nimble feet and a heart bigger than himself.

15 **John Whiteley.** John was the perfect gentleman on the field, a pure footballer who, despite the ferocity of a match, could walk off the pitch with his arm around my shoulder, as he did after only my third game of

Rugby League, giving me advice on to how to approach my new code. John was the brains behind the mighty Hull pack of the 1950s and 1960s.

The players of my playing days and especially those who continued in active service on the pitch until the mid-1970s possibly experienced more dramatic rule changes than at any time since the early days when League, at the turn of the century, changed its shape from Union. Players were initially introduced to the four-tackle law in 1966 and then, six years later, to the six-tackle law – two rule changes which limited the number of tackles from which a side could retain the ball before a scrum was called. Such an innovation was eventually to revolutionise the style of Rugby League as players became conversant with playing under these strictures. However, during the 1960s and the early 1970s few players really mastered those laws. Most players were coached in their formative years under the old unlimited-tackle law and had played the bulk of their careers under it. So the result was only too often a hybrid form of the style of the previous era and that of today. There was much frantic handling, though halves like Murphy and Hardisty were moving the ball out wider at the expense of the close forward exchanges. More broken-field running developed and there was a general opening out of play to the threequarters but the packs tended to be only slightly lighter though faster versions of the previous era.

Two noticeable aspects of play developed in the form of the kicking duties in a team. The incidence of scrums was in fact cut down as sides, not favouring the scrummage at the conclusion of the sixth tackle, kicked aimlessly upfield to clear their lines and we were treated, sadly, to the sight of virtually any player booting the ball in the direction of the opposition, often without much thought. Ironically, when the drop goal was reduced to 1 point in 1974 we saw an increase in them, rather than a decrease, thanks to the insistence that, after six tackles, an attacking team should never leave their opponents' 25-yards area without a point. Players like Alex Murphy and, later, Harry Pinner became experts in the art of dropping goals.

My side from the years 1961–72 would thus have to be equipped to play the game under both the unlimited- and the limited-tackle laws and for that reason there is a mixture of speed and tenacity in the pack. Indeed the tackling ability of my pack would, I am sure, render the backs obsolete but with Billy Boston and Nick Sullivan on the wings there would be few openings on the flanks either. The team is, above all, a resilient professional outfit whose players were all 'winners' in their day. Whether they would beat the past or the present is again debatable though my ego would like to say that they would.

1981–88. 'The Commentator'

Mick Burke (Widnes, Oldham); Martin Offiah (Widnes), Garry Schofield (Hull, Leeds), David Stephenson (Wigan, Leeds), Joe Lydon (Widnes, Wigan); Shaun Edwards (Wigan), Andy Gregory (Widnes, Warrington, Wigan); Lee Crooks (Hull, Leeds), Kevin Beardmore (Castleford), Kevin Ward (Castleford), Andy Goodway (Oldham, Wigan), Steve Norton (Hull), Ellery Hanley (Bradford Northern, Wigan)

Substitutes Tony Myler (Widnes), Harry Pinner (St Helens, Bradford Northern)

1 **Mick Burke.** Mick was one of the most talented youngsters I have ever had the pleasure of coaching; even at school his sense of timing both in attack and defence was exceptional. Though heavily built, often weighing up to 14 stone, few could outpace him at full-back, such was his

positional play. Having played Rugby Union for England Schools and Waterloo, his catching of the ball under pressure was well practised when facing high 'bombs' in League. His handling abilities made him an instant success at Widnes where in his first season, 1978–79, he broke the club's goal-kicking and points-scoring records.

2 **Martin Offiah.** This sensational winger topped the Rugby League's try-scoring charts with 44 tries for Widnes in his first season in 1987–88. And, for good measure, he headed the try-scorers in Australasia during the 1988 Great Britain tour. A signing from Rosslyn Park RU, Martin is blessed with pure speed, a devastating swerve, and a determination to score tries. Though comparatively new to the game, and with much to learn, his raw talent already marks him as a player of the greatest potential.

3 **Garry Schofield.** Christened 'the Poacher' by the media, Garry has the uncanny ability to be always in the right place at the right time as when, in the second Test against New Zealand in 1985, at the age of only eighteen, he scored 4 tries to equal Billy Boston's feat thirty-one years before. His timing of the interception, always a difficult ploy to perform, is uncanny and has led to many spectacular long distance try-scoring efforts. In defence, his penchant for the crash tackle on his opposite centre is all the more effective for his speed off the mark with the result that he has been welcomed by the Balmain and Western Suburbs clubs for summer stints in the Sydney League.

4 **David Stephenson.** David is my 'Mr Dependable' of Rugby League. I have watched this player since his Arnold School RU days and, though rarely electrifying the crowds, he is the consistently polished performer whom teams rely on. Solid in defence, a strong runner, and a centre who invariably plays to his winger, David always gives an air of consistency and professionalism to a side.

5 **Joe Lydon**. Since his inauspicious start to international Rugby League on the 1984 tour of Australasia, Joe has toughened up physically yet has lost none of the dynamic pace and ability to swerve round defenders. His two tries for Widnes against his present club, Wigan, at Wembley in 1984 illustrated his opportunism and speed, attributes which make him well worth the £100,000 fee paid by Wigan for his services.

6 **Shaun Edwards**. Having served an apprenticeship following his record £35,000 signing for Wigan on his seventeenth birthday, Shaun is now fulfilling all the promise he showed as a schoolboy. He is a dedicated trainer who works at his weaknesses and strengths, has blistering pace over the first thirty yards (so vital for a stand-off), and has a keen knowledge of the game's tactics. I have been especially pleased to see him bring the art of kicking back into the game with his shrewd use of the grubber and chip kicks.

7 **Andy Gregory**. A pugnacious, cheeky scrum-half who, with sleeves rolled up, likes to take on the whole of the opposition. His chatter and banter urge on his own teammates and prove a nuisance and a distraction to the opposition. He is keen to run at the opposition from the scrums in the manner of previous eras.

8 **Lee Crooks**. Lee made his debut in Test football at the age of eighteen in 1982 and already seems a veteran, such is his experience both in Britain with Hull and Leeds and in Australia with Western Suburbs and Balmain. He is a rarity among props today in that he is a superb ball distributor, a skill which probably accounts for his world record transfer fee of £172,000 from Hull to Leeds.

9 **Kevin Beardmore**. Kevin is a hooker and a good footballer in the mould of Egan and Ward. A wholehearted lad who puts all his energy into the game's eighty minutes and occasionally steals the glory with well taken tries from a

play-the-ball situation. I have always been impressed with his serious attitude to the game.

10 **Kevin Ward**. This 16-stone prop matured throughout the 1980s before hitting peak form with the Manly club in Sydney in the summer of 1987. Kevin likes to drive the ball upfield in determined fashion, is a strong tackler, and plays the type of game now expected of a modern prop.

11 **Andy Goodway**. I have found Andy to be a temperamental player but when on form there is no better runner to break up an opposition's defence. His outstanding form on the 1984 tour of Australasia impressed me, as did the intensity of his application to his own personal fitness.

12 **Steve Norton**. Steve is the 'wild card' in my pack of forwards, being a player with the vision to see situations others cannot. His ball distribution has always been of the highest order, nor was he lacking in pace when he was needed to finish a movement himself. Like Vince Karalius, Steve invariably held the ball well away from his body in order to slip passes to those in support.

13 **Ellery Hanley**. Ellery is an outstanding example of the modern loose forward. An individualist, an exciting runner and a prolific scorer of tries (no less than 128 in the last three seasons), Ellery likes to roam far and wide away from the scrums and as Graham Lowe, his Wigan coach, confirms 'does his own thing'. He can break up play with one direct run at the opposition, such is his strength.

14 **Tony Myler**. Tall for a stand-off, Tony can remain upright in the tackle and still offload the ball to those in support. He is a thinker when on attack, always looking to vary his own play and that of the Widnes or Great Britain team; in defence he rarely shirks a tackle.

15 **Harry Pinner**. Harry is one of a rare species in the 1980s, a constructive, ball-playing loose forward. Though small for a forward Harry is able to dictate a game by virtue of his defence-splitting passes and tactical kicks to touch. With over eighty 1-point goals to his credit Harry has proved himself to be an outstanding drop-kick specialist.

The teams of the 1980s contain only players who have been coached under the limited-tackle law and, as such, all are conversant now with its demands. Most players, too, were quickly made aware of the demands of the new handover law, introduced in 1983, under which a team in possession, after six tackles, must hand the ball over to the opposition. This law, and the increase in a try's value to 4 points, has placed the emphasis in Rugby League more than ever on attack. And, if the experimental laws in use last season are continued (players being forced to retire five metres behind the scrum and the insistence on only one marker at a play-the-ball) then the code will become even faster and more open than it is at present. The speed of the game has demanded much fitter players, especially forwards who must be fast, all-purpose players. Though the props, such as Lee Crooks and Kevin Ward, are still big men, their constructive ball-playing abilities are not so necessary now, as all forwards, even the loose forward, must be able to run, tackle and pass. The big strong forwards still need to absorb the tackles but, with scrums now down to as few as an average of sixteen a match, many players now pack down at prop or second row according to the coach's preference. With fewer scrums, the loose forward has become, like Ellery Hanley, a gifted runner, tackler, and try scorer but not necessarily a constructive ball handler.

The whole shift of emphasis has, to my mind, moved away from the ball players in the pack to the half-backs, who are now the key players under the handover law. Andy Gregory, Shaun Edwards, and their like will, with more broken-field play, handle the ball more than anyone else on the pitch, and most of the tactical play will stem from them. Both will probably make less tackles than their counterparts in previous eras as they make most of their moves away from the scrums, though David Hulme (Widnes), in the stand off-position, registered an amazing thirty-four tackles in that historic third Test victory by Great Britain over Australia in 1988. However, they will have to develop a tactical kicking game which is now very much a part of the plans of any modern coach who seeks ploys to use the ball on the sixth tackle, rather than hand it over to the opposition.

A combination of short grubber kicks, tactical kicks to the touchlines, or long penetrating kicks deep to the corners of the pitch can punish an opposition. I have seen no better example of such an effective kicking game than that carried out by Great Britain, again in that third Test victory over Australia. Andy Gregory, with his short lateral kicking to touch, and Paul Loughlin, from the centre, with his powerful long-kicks behind the Australian full-back, Garry Jack, upset the Kangaroos' rhythm and contained them in a vice-like grip in their own half. Sadly, with regard to the art of kicking, I do feel that the introduction of the differential penalty in 1976 for technical offences at the scrums, though happily cutting down the opportunities to gain 2 points from a penalty by virtue of a relatively minor offence, has helped to bring about a decline in goal-kicking. It is customary today to see two or even three players take kicks at goal for the same team in a match. Few teams seem to have an outstanding kicker in the mould of Bernard Ganley, Kel Coslett, or David Watkins. It is perhaps significant that there are four recognised goal-kickers – Burke, Stephenson, Lydon, and Crooks – in my team as well as Edwards and Pinner who have also met with some success.

However, whatever may be the merits of the three teams I have selected and whatever the arguments over the superiority of an individual era, the importance of that élite band of players who make up the Great Britain team is now greater than ever. In a world of mass media exposure of sport and with the accompanying glare of television, the image of Rugby League, especially the home-grown variety, is all important. Sponsors are attracted to successful products, uncommitted supporters like to ally themselves to success whatever the sport, and youngsters seek to emulate the sporting heroes portrayed in the media. Since Britain's last Test series win over Australia in 1970 their performances have ranged from the abysmal to the promising. Other nations have stolen a march but hopefully, after the promise shown on that last Australian tour, as we approach the close of the 1980s, we might be on the way to reasserting ourselves at international level. It is vital that we do so, for the projection of a successful national team is the recipe for a thriving sport in the 1990s. Star players come and go, playing styles change, but the public's attitude to, and respect for, Rugby League, whether in the northern or the home counties stands or falls on its performance at international level.

9

New Frontiers

Rugby League must develop more international competition, create new international teams in virgin territory and consolidate the code in areas like France, New Zealand, and Australia. Indeed the need to make Rugby League a truly international sport has been a main topic of discussion for the last three decades. At amateur level the sport has gained a tiny foothold in Canada and America, is in its formative stages in the Pacific Islands of Western Samoa, Norfolk Island, and the Cook Islands and at last looks to be succeeding in the predominantly Rugby Union islands of Fiji and Tonga. Indeed Tonga, having supported a six-club RL league throughout the 1988 season, took part in the Rugby League Pacific Cup in October/November 1988 despite the curious intervention of the Minister of Police, A'Kau'ola, a prominent Rugby Union sup- porter.

Four Tongan policemen had their applications for leave to play in the Pacific Cup blocked by the Minister. However, the success of the RL venture seems assured as the first president of the 13-a-side game in Tonga is none other than the King's youngest son, Ulukalalu Larake-ta. With such influence in high circles and the example of Widnes's latest pack star from Tonga, Emosi Koloto, to set before the young Tongan players, I do not see Union as a hindrance to the League code's future development. Fiji has, in the past, provided the professional game with the likes of Joe Levula and Jo Ravouvou, who enjoyed fame at Rochdale Hornets in the 1960s, while the New Zealand Test players, Fred Ah Kuoi, James Leuluai, Mark Elia, and Olsen Filipaina, all Samoan born, bear testimony to what talent the island can produce.

League has so infiltrated the universities of Scotland and Wales that both (plus an Irish universities team) were able to take their places in the recent Students World Cup, held in the summer of 1989. Such developments, admittedly still in their infancy, are encouraging to those of us who have for years argued the need for overseas expansion of the League code and for the need to enlarge the international numbers of the family. Now in the professional ranks, where the sport captures the public's imagination, all sorts of promising initiatives are coming from the International Board.

Any visitor to Sydney or Brisbane need only stay in his hotel room and watch television for a couple of hours at any time over a weekend to realise that Rugby League is not only in a thoroughly healthy state in Australia but looks to have a very promising future there. Though Newtown, a Sydney suburb club, was forced out of the Sydney Premiership League because of financial problems in 1983, the addition of Illawarra and Canberra, both cities well outside the Sydney city boundaries, were the first steps towards the realisation of an all-Australian league. The addition of Brisbane Broncos, the Gold Coast Giants, and Newcastle Knights, bringing the present Sydney League strength to sixteen teams in 1988, was another stage in the development of what is probably the strongest and wealthiest Rugby League organisation in the world. So strong is the game at club level that each club in the Sydney League would put our own soccer giants, such as Manchester United, Liverpool, and Arsenal, into the shade when it comes to wealth and supporter involvement.

St George, a club founded in 1921 and producing some of the all-time greats of Australian Rugby League in Norman Provan, Graeme Langlands, John Raper, and Reg Gasnier, are a typical example of the strength and financial viability of the Sydney League. Controlled by a nine-man board of directors, St George Ltd., as the club is known since it became a public company in 1987, has over 49,000 members paying only A$15 (about £7) per year for their membership. And if we look at the sports available for those members – over seventeen major sports including bowls, cricket, baseball, squash, billiards, and their own country golf club – we can deduce why so many pay such a small fee to be members of the club. When we consider the entertainment facilities within the huge complex of buildings and grounds we can see how cheap that membership fee is. There are games rooms featuring darts, snooker, and indoor bowls, two cinemas, four restaurants ranging from high-class Chinese to a fast-service bistro, an auditorium (for variety shows) which seats over 1000 people, countless lounge bars and of course rooms full of hundreds of poker gambling machines. Oh yes, and a Rugby League club organising teams from Under-8s in the district league right up to the premier side containing such internationals as Craig Young and Wally Fullerton-Smith.

Though the rugby section is not entirely funded by the St George League club it has been taken over by the vast profits accruing from the catering and of course the poker machines. From a financial turnover of over £2m on the restaurants and bars and of almost £5m from the poker machines, the club in 1987 returned a typical profit of almost £1.75m. This is a staggering sum for a sporting club, out of which almost £400,000 is distributed to the Rugby League club for general playing needs. When Penfolds Wines' sponsorship of about £100,000 a season is added, plus other individual match sponsorships, then it is not impossible for the rugby club to receive something like £750,000 a season before a single spectator even passes through the turnstiles at the Kogarah Oval, the home of St George. When one considers that the average home gates will be no more than the typical gates at St Helens or Wigan, then it is patently obvious that the strength of most of the teams in the Sydney League lies heavily in returns from the poker machines and other entertainments. Incentive prizes of watches, television sets, trips to Hawaii, and even a free champagne fountain, from which gamblers may drink as much as they like, are on hand to tempt more dollars from the punters' pockets.

Not all clubs are able to utilise the profits from the poker machines. The Brisbane Broncos, the new Queensland club, are denied access to such sums since poker machines are banned in that state. Nevertheless the Brisbane Broncos' financial backing is equal to that of St George by virtue of huge sponsorship deals with a famous Queensland company, Power Brewing, who have pledged sponsorship of £1.5m between 1988–90. The addition of the three clubs from outside Sydney in the 1988 season proved a huge success, with the Newcastle Knights averaging almost 20,000 spectators a match in their inaugural season. Both the Gold Coast Giants, who have one of the biggest entertainment and restaurant complexes in Australia, and Newcastle, who are currently planning a major club and entertainment complex on the local waterfront, proved financially viable and enjoyed considerable success in their first season. The Brisbane Broncos rapidly became the focal point for the Queenslanders' fanatical appreciation of Rugby League at Lang Park and, led by the incomparable Wally Lewis, they too enjoyed a successful baptism in the 1988 season, but their exit left the Brisbane League in some disarray.

Outside Sydney, throughout New South Wales and Queensland, the various area leagues in town and country districts are very strong and in Sydney there has even been recent talk of plans to bring back a second division, such is the strength of other Sydney teams like Wentworthville, Mount Pritchard, and Guildford. Yet in Brisbane there is little doubt that the League has been denuded of quality players, financial opportunities and, above all, spectator interest. In that first season in the Sydney League the Brisbane Broncos attracted a 20,000 gate to Lang Park for their match with St George. Yet the whole of the once thriving Brisbane League of ten teams could only produce a total average gate of 7000 spectators for five matches on that same weekend. Of seventy sponsors involved in Rugby League in Brisbane, over sixty are associated only with the Broncos.

When the idea of the Brisbane Broncos taking part in the Sydney League was first mooted it was thought that just such a setback to Brisbane RL might happen and it was agreed that 30 per cent of all the Broncos' profits would go to the Queensland Rugby League for distribution to the Brisbane division generally. Indeed, such were the financial problems of the struggling Brisbane clubs that at the end of the Broncos' first season the chairman of the Australian Rugby League was asked to chair a meeting between the two bodies while the Brisbane League sought £120,000 compensation for loss of spectators.

Whatever the teething troubles in Brisbane, Ken Arthurson's vision of Rugby League becoming a national code at professional level in Australia seems on target except for one area. In Northern Territories the game continues to prosper with thriving leagues built round the major cities like Darwin, while in Western Australia, and especially in Perth, the development is so strong that plans are already afoot to include a team, based in Perth, in the

Sydney League within the next five years. Sadly, in Melbourne and Victoria, the home of the Australian Rules game, Rugby League, apart from a healthy amateur league of twelve teams at first and reserve grades, has made little headway and looks unlikely to do so for some considerable time yet. Melbourne's insular attitude to sport is the biggest obstacle. The media will give coverage to no alien football code, while Victoria and Tasmania are the only states which do not enjoy live coverage of Rugby League. It is rare for even the League scores to appear in the newspapers. One would imagine that the reader is on another planet such is the lack of league coverage – deliberate, I may add – in this part of Australia. Hopefully, things will improve.

When I first visited New Zealand in 1968 to take part in the World Cup tournament, Rugby League was barely tolerated by the sporting public there, compared to their first love, Rugby Union. In 1984, when the Kiwis won all three League Tests against Great Britain for the first time in their history, the League code was suddenly appreciated. When I last returned, as a television commentator and scribe in 1988, I was made fully aware that Rugby League was not only admired on a wider scale but was respected as never before for the achievements of the Kiwi national team. There is no doubt that the deeds of Kevin Iro, Kurt Sorensen, Mark Graham, and Clayton Friend have elevated them alongside their Union counterparts, John Kirwan, Wayne Shelford, and Joe Stanley in the New Zealand sporting public's consciousness. There is no doubt that the profile of the League code is at a very high level and it is with the clubs and the provincial teams that the greatest progress has been made.

My most recent trip to New Zealand with the 1988 Great Britain touring side amply illustrated the public's thirst for the game now, especially in the Union strongholds of Wellington and Christchurch. The enthusiasm for League in Auckland has always been high, and the record-breaking crowd of 45,000 for the World Cup final between New Zealand and Australia, incidentally held at the home of the All Blacks Union side, Eden Park, was indicative of the extent of that interest. But in Wellington, where the ground proved too small for a Great Britain tour match, and in Christchurch, where every ticket was sold for the first time in fifty years at the Addington Showground, showed the impact now being made by Rugby League. One exciting development at club level throughout all the area leagues, and especially in Auckland, Wellington, and Christchurch, where the major leagues are centred, is in the area of professionalism. New Zealand Rugby League has always been strictly amateur, with only the stars who played overseas for British or Australian clubs receiving payment while abroad. The news that James Leuluai, the old Hull and Kiwi centre, has recently been receiving payments for a two-season spell with the Petone club in Wellington, and that others such as Kevin Iro, Wayne Wallace and Shane Horo have been playing to contracts, indicates that the code is now becoming fully professional. That professionalism, which will surely spread throughout New Zealand RL, is indicative of the increase in spectator interest and in sponsorship by major companies such as Lion Red Breweries and Adidas.

Such is the spectator interest and the boom in attendances at Test matches that already plans are in hand to utilise some of Rugby Union's top venues for Great Britain's tour of New Zealand in the summer of 1990.

The New Zealand Rugby League chairman, George Rainey, has already had discussions with the governing bodies of Lancaster Park, Christchurch, Eden Park, Auckland, and the Showgrounds in Palmerston North. Nor is the huge interest in League confined to the grounds, as can be seen from the fact that, for that last World Cup final, a mammoth television viewing figure of over 1 million was achieved – a figure involving roughly one in three of the country's total potential audience.

Progress has also been made by Rugby League's latest international recruit, Papua New Guinea, where the game is truly the country's national sport and, indeed, the object of remarkable fanaticism. The promotion of club rugby, especially in Port Moresby, proceeds at an exciting rate but it is in the skills of their national sides that Papua New Guinea has come of age. Though suffering heavy defeats in Britain, New Zealand, and Australia because of the Kumals' problems with the climate and their diminutive forwards, they are none the less providing a difficult team to beat at home in their own hot, humid climate. Support for the game is limited only by the small size of their stadiums. Anyone seeing the spectators perched in trees and sitting on top of corrugated tin roofs surrounding the grounds at Port Moresby and Lae, when the Great Britain tourists visited them in 1988, were left in no doubt about their total conversion to the League code on the island.

Sadly, much nearer home, our closest rivals, France, have experienced severe problems during the 1980s, so much so that the game, by the end of the 1986–87 season, was in danger of becoming a backwater of French sport. Indeed, the very existence of French Rugby League was in doubt as their governing body struggled with financial liabilities, constant bickering between the governing body and the clubs themselves and the desertion of many leading players and coaches to Rugby Union where, despite the amateur ethos, playing wages and contracts were often much higher than those being paid in League. The situation became farcical when the supposedly amateur Union clubs of France were, in the January of 1988, busy chasing France's newly emerging League stars, Gilles Dumas,

Jacques Moliner and David Fraisse, with tempting personal offers of £30,000 or more. However, following an emergency meeting in Carcassonne with David Oxley, the chief executive of the Rugby Football League and an International Board member, financial help was found, harmony restored in the management of the sport, and, over the past two seasons, we have seen some improvement in League's fortunes there.

At last, Rugby League matches are now shown on French television with the result that clubs like Le Pontet, Carcassonne, and Catalan XIII are attracting sponsorship again. At international level France is aiming to reassert itself by getting as much competition as it can at top level. A short tour of Great Britain in October 1988 by their national side, playing Warrington, Halifax, and Cumbria, and a short tour of France by the Penrith club from Australia, have again given their players a real sense of international competition. And perhaps the most promising indication for the future of Rugby League in France and elsewhere on the Continent has been the appointment of their former coach, Tas Baitieri, as the game's European development officer. Already in Holland, where games have been played between clubs from Holland and Hull, and where an Easter festival of Rugby League, based on the Drechtstreek club, near Amsterdam, proved such a success; in Spain and the Basque country where they have regularly taken the BBC's televised match coverage; in Germany where a team from Bocholt took part in the Drechtstreek Easter festival; and in Italy where the game thrived in the early 1950s, there are signs that expansion could take place if given Baitieri's full attention. But the biggest capture for the League code must remain Japan and America where at last there appear to be stirrings of interest.

The failure of the much heralded 1988 World Club

championship to take place was a severe setback to international expansion. And the Australians, who believed there was insufficient time to stage the championship, followed by the final in Tokyo, and who pulled the plug on the competition, must be taken to task. Japan would have been a bold move and one which would have given Rugby League the central stage on television. It would have been even more important in attracting financial backing and player and spectator interest in order to introduce the League code to Japan. The Japanese have a strong liking for Rugby Union but because of their short stature they are invariably at the receiving end of heavy defeats against European clubs. Since League demands much less bulk from its players, and relies more on running, passing, and tackling, it was thought that the Japanese would be sympathetic to the introduction of the League game. The big finance houses of Japan and the vast wealth of their major companies is also a huge attraction to a sport looking for essential sponsorship before world expansion can take place. The next twelve months should determine whether the Australians will share Britain's enthusiasm for a journey to the Far East. They must, for I firmly believe that the 13-a-side code would be an ideal Japanese import. Hopefully the challenge match in October 1989 between the British League champions and the Australian Grand Final winners will lead to a major game there.

The past twelve months have also seen the mood of internationalism strike at the other major country in League's sights – the USA – and again with considerable optimism. Thanks to the staging of an Australian State of Origin match between New South Wales and Queensland at Long Beach, California in August 1987, Rugby League established a toehold. A 12,000 crowd at the match, extensive TV coverage of Australian and British matches on cable TV following the event, and the appointment of development officers to work in the US universities and high schools provided much satisfaction to those, like me, who have long urged expansion into America. With many fine athletes unable to hold down places in the professional American Football leagues, and with the Americans' natural reluctance to involve themselves wholeheartedly in any amateur sport like Rugby Union, it has been clear for a long time that conditions have been ripe for the introduction of Rugby League.

In June of this year a serious attempt was begun to introduce by 1992 the League code at professional level in eight major US cities. An exhibition game in Milwaukee, Wisconsin, between Wigan and Warrington, which attracted considerable interest both locally and nationally via cable TV, was seen as the catalyst by interested parties in the States to the formation of an RL league. It is too early yet to assess the full impact made by this exciting venture but there is little doubt that, at last, there is a real desire to expand Rugby League's frontiers. And where better to succeed with a fast, tough physical sport than America? Should such ideas be realised, alongside the development of Rugby League in American universities, then Rugby League will have a future in the US. And I have no doubt that the country's financing and marketing expertise of sporting events will extend Rugby League's horizons even further.

All these developments in the last few years have come after lengthy periods of much talking but little action. At last, however, there is a genuine determination to succeed on the part of three major Rugby League playing countries – Great Britain, Australia, and New Zealand – and I do not think it is simply coincidence that all three governing bodies are now led by men of vision, with the strength to encourage radical changes in their domestic game and positively seek international expansion.

10

Into the 20th Century

Great Britain was the last of the major League playing nations to streamline its governing body from an unwieldy thirty-four-man council, with representatives from each club, to a five-man board of directors. Already, after only a year, there are signs of renewed vigour in the sport. And David Oxley, the chief executive of the five-man board, sees the new administrative body as being the catalyst for an optimistic future in Britain. When the vote was cast for the proposal to abandon the old Rugby League Council as the premier governing body and to introduce a much smaller executive arm, the voting was 32 votes to 2 in favour of the change, only the representatives from Batley and Swinton resisting reform. The five elected members, who do not retain their seats on the full council, will serve for three years under David Oxley, meet every week, and report four times a year to the full council, who will still meet as a 'sounding board' for the game.

No longer will the weak hold back the strong and, as events have proved during the past season, matters of urgency will be dealt with much more quickly and efficiently. Though there has been some criticism, notably from Swinton, that the members of the executive body, as representatives of clubs, will still have the interests of those clubs uppermost in their minds, David Oxley sees the new body growing away from club connections. 'Though members were, in the first instance, elected from the Rugby League Council by the Council, I believe it will not be long before two members will be appointed from outside the clubs.'

That would be a welcome move, ridding the game of petty club jealousies which have plagued the code in the past. But, as David Oxley indicates, the new executive members will be taking on virtually full-time jobs which may well require considerable reimbursement.

'Each member of the five-man board has been given a specific responsibility, for example, finance, grounds or marketing, and though, at first, the members may be retired people or professional men able to give their time freely to the job, in the near future they may be paid salaries for their services.'

Whether they are eventually paid or not is immaterial as long as the new management panel is efficient and effective, as it needs to be as we approach an age which is even more complex for the world of sport. The purchase of the building next door to the Rugby League headquarters in Leeds for the use of more full-time administrators is evidence of the workload now being undertaken off the field and is yet another step towards good management.

David Oxley is insistent that the cultivation of the media, and making the country as a whole, and especially London, aware of Rugby League is one of the prime tasks of the new controlling body. It is surprising to learn that, though the game in recent seasons has been Britain's second largest spectator sport after soccer, it actually has fewer participants on the field than women's soccer. David Oxley admits that, in terms of players, Rugby League is a mini sport and, with only five major nations playing the code in comparison to the 110 which encourage Rugby Union, the game probably gets the media coverage it deserves. RL must do all it can to win the attention given to other sports if its expansion is to continue, aiming particularly at those newspapers which have moved away from the north for more secure bases in London and the south.

David Oxley has said: 'There is a strong feeling that we must open up a London office or commercial offices in the south to complement our headquarters in Leeds. We must be in daily contact with television and we must be lobbying the press regularly from within London where all the sports editors are now based and who determine the extent of an individual sport's coverage in their newspaper.' Oxley also sees the development of offices in London as helping to encourage the growth at amateur and professional levels in the south. 'We must support the London amateur game and Fulham by a genuine presence in the south of England. With the new coaching and development officer, Ken Johnson, we must build up, as quickly as possible, the amateur side of Rugby League so as to be able to install another professional club in London as soon as is practicable.'

This is a sensible aim, for the presence of a second professional club in the area would do much to increase the media's awareness of the game, provide competition and a spur for Fulham, while both would gain respectability and strength from each other's presence. Admittedly, in recent seasons the Rugby League Council has been aware that investment has to be made in new clubs, especially in the south, if they are to thrive. When a supermarket chain, such as Sainsbury's, opens a new outlet the central body advises and finances the new offspring. Such should be the case with Rugby League. David Oxley agrees. 'We have deviated from the rules to help Fulham in the past with travel subsidies and an increased quota of overseas players but we do need the rivalry and competitiveness of another club in London. But our priority must be to encourage the amateur game in the London area, especially in the schools, where we must launch a big effort to regain the foothold we lost a few years back.'

David Oxley has to tread carefully in this area for there are still people in Rugby League who regard developments in London as a waste of money compared with the need to consolidate further the game in the north. Like the dinosaurs of old, such species are highly dangerous and, like the dinosaurs, must be allowed to disappear or be wiped out as quickly as possible. Nevertheless there is a need for a balanced programme of consolidation in the north and enlightened expansion elsewhere. In David Oxley's opinion the links between professional clubs and local authorities will increase with the appointment of jointly-funded development officers. But clubs will be expected to become more professional in their approach. As has been the case in Australia for a considerable number of years now, 'the governing body will make the clubs more professional by setting standards. Already there is a strong body of opinion which believes that clubs wishing to join the first division must have a full-time secretary or manager, have installed floodlights, have a licensed capacity of not less than 10,000, and must be able to run an Alliance side. If they do not comply with those regulations then, even if they are the second division champions, they might not be allowed to play in the first division.'

Hence, the onus for the further development of the traditional clubs is to be left to themselves, but with more than gentle prodding from the centre. However, there will be no compulsory winding-up orders should there be a need for retraction or amalgamation of some of the weaker clubs. In neighbouring communities like Batley and Dewsbury, where the size of the population may not be able to support professional Rugby League in both towns, we may in the future see some amalgamation or even retraction of clubs. But if that happens it will not be at the insistence of the Rugby League executive. Indeed, I believe help will always be given, if it is thought worthwhile, to stave off a crisis at a struggling club. David Oxley was most insistent that, 'Though the code must be streamlined and taken into the 21st century as a thoroughly professional sport, any retraction that comes about will never take place as the result of an edict by the governing body. Our small clubs are tremendously resilient and one can only admire the tenacity of people. We have had very little natural wastage in recent times.' What wastage there has been has sadly occurred at newer clubs like Kent Invicta and Cardiff which enjoyed brief lives in the early 1980s.

David Oxley admits that the game learned much from those ventures but does not want to discourage further development. The aim for the future must be more expansion, but with the expansion much more controlled than before by the Rugby Football League.

'We have learned the lesson that you cannot expand at professional level unless you first have a solid, vibrant amateur basis to build on. It need only be five years in an area like Bristol or Gloucester but the amateur development must come first. Any consortium wishing to introduce Rugby League will be subjected to the most stringent tests. There must be a sound amateur base acting as the catalyst to a professional club and those who wish to be in charge will be screened as to their financial integrity. Then we will have a thorough marketing back-up and people will be employed to look at the target area to see whether Rugby League is really viable there.'

This is a commonsense approach and one which should ensure regulated future expansion but, as David Oxley has continually stressed, 'We must first get the game right at youth level before we can make real progress.' It is indeed heartening to know that the RFL intends to make this a priority, though, like myself, Oxley acknowledges the massive difficulties now facing sport in schools. It is all the more interesting, therefore, to note that the RFL see schools as a first point of contact with the game and a point of contact which can be developed, if necessary, through the local amateur club. Says Oxley, 'Schools are now more willing than ever to accept and welcome our development officers but, once the interest has been kindled, if the school is unable to organise the sport, then we must have a structure in place for the 7-year-olds and upwards to take advantage of the enthusiasm that has been generated.' The youngsters in the smaller units of primary schools are possibly the best targets to aim at in both the north and south; and a further sign of the RFL's efficiency in this field can be seen in a recent policy decision.

'Most youngsters these days in junior schools,' David Oxley explains, 'are taught by women and we are encouraging as many female teachers as possible to take our coaching courses. Of course they must be able to inculcate the right qualities in the children, not generate a win-at-all-costs mentality.'

Hopefully if enthusiasm of these youngsters is captured then the work of the national development officer, Tom O'Donovan, whose principal brief is to strengthen and expand the League code in the high schools and sixth-form colleges, will be made a good deal easier. And, in turn, David Oxley's hopes for a rapid development of the game at university level will be achieved all the earlier. Owing to the fact that universities change their population every three years there is an urgent need to provide continuity in administration by the Rugby Football League having its own full-time professional universities development officer. We will, I hope, be the first sport to achieve this. After London, the development of Rugby League in the universities and colleges is easily the most important of our priorities.

It is a blessing that conflict in the other area of youth rugby, between the professional clubs' Colts and the amateur Under-19 sides, has been settled satisfactorily, though, as David Oxley explains, the friction between the two governing bodies was much less than had been depicted. 'Between the officers of the professional and the amateur bodies there has always been considerable friendship and mutual respect. The issue tended to become emotive and grew out of all proportion to its importance. The Colts system was on too narrow a base whereas BARLA's youth policy was always too wide and fragmented. Now, with a joint, coherent policy between the two bodies, with funds from the Rugby League Foundation, and with more money to come from a development known as the 'Friends of the Foundation', groups of businesses, each of which will give £1000 in return for big match concessions, the future looks assured.'

The situation facing Oxley now is totally different from the one that faced him in the bleak days of his appointment as secretary-general in 1974. Such is the current strength of the code in Britain that at last he and his governing body can turn their attention to the expansion of the game world-wide, even injecting finance into such ventures. Oxley has long been an advocate of international expansion and has played a leading role in recent attempts to take the game to America. But I am sure he would agree with me that, for the first time, the International Board has been blessed with a director-general, the Australian Ken Arthurson, also the executive chairman of the Australian Rugby Football League, who is a genuine supporter of international development as well as being an administrator with a remarkable vision for the needs of his own country. Like David Oxley in Great Britain, Ken Arthurson was frustrated for years in the New South Wales Rugby League hierarchy, of which he is still chairman, by having to deal with an even larger governing body and one equally as parochial. Forty-seven members, representing clubs and areas throughout Australia, tried to direct Rugby League policy and, as Ken Arthurson indicates, not without bias on their part.

'That large board simply did not work for most representatives simply voted in line with their club's interests, which inevitably held back the progress of the game. The nine-man board which came into operation when the New South Wales RL became a corporate body five years ago has worked well and is now a huge success.' Arthurson then stepped up as executive chairman of the ARFL thus retaining the chairmanship of the NSW Rugby League.

One advantage which the Australian board of control has over the British, and one which David Oxley also supports in principle, is the inclusion of two members from outside Rugby League with no vested interest in the game itself. In Australia, they are men who combine enthusiasm for the game with a shrewd business sense. One example of what the new-look Australian board has achieved is massive television coverage of the game throughout all the states of Australia with an equally massive revenue to Australian Rugby League.

Television, on account of the vast distances between cities in Australia, is the vital medium for promoting the code and there is no doubt that almost saturation coverage of the game has done much to raise the profile of the sport and bring in considerable extra revenue to the clubs. As Ken Arthurson points out, 'When the new board renegotiated television contracts and organised Monday and Friday evening television matches, we would never have got these proposals through the old governing body for there were serious misgivings in certain clubs. Now, the whole television format is welcomed, we have double the financial return and have taken the code to areas never before exposed to Rugby League.'

Indeed, the Melbourne RFL plan to stage a State of Origin match in Melbourne next season after a record £25m deal with Channel 10. With the sale of those rights they now have the capital to expand nationally in Australia.

Thanks to the supreme powers the Australian governing body has acquired, Australia was the first country to be able to lay down a set of minimum standards required of the clubs who wished to be admitted to their premier league competition, the Winfield Cup. These basic standards, in Ken Arthurson's opinion, are now responsible for the current strength of the league and are being copied by the authorities in Great Britain. 'All the clubs have to spend a minimum of £25,000 a year on the propagation of junior and schools rugby in their area and each district must support at least 100 junior teams, apart from schoolboys. The clubs must also have the ability to promote a high degree of sponsorship and generate considerable funds from it.'

The Australian board's insistence on basic standards has proved successful in the upgrading of the quality of clubs in the Winfield Cup and most have become corporate bodies, no longer fully part of the Leagues clubs but still closely allied to these vast social clubs which encourage Rugby League football in the district. Though two of the recent additions to the Winfield Cup competition, the Brisbane Broncos and the Gold Coast Giants, are privately owned it is a trend which Ken Arthurson does not welcome. 'I may be old fashioned but I am a little apprehensive about the matter of private ownership. Problems can be created when the owner loses interest in, or becomes disillusioned with, his purchase. Anyone who thinks he will make money out of Rugby League is wrong; it is a very expensive hobby.'

Whatever misgivings Ken Arthurson might have there is ample evidence that the policies of the past few years are now reaping dividends. Crowds increased by 40 per cent in the 1988 season and were set to go even higher in 1989 as Rugby League became the only sport in Australia at which the crowds are on the increase.

However, Peter Moore, the much respected Canterbury Bankstown director and a member of the Australian board, is worried by the situation in Sydney. 'I can see the amalgamations of clubs in the inner city, maybe ten years down the track. The crowds supporting city-teams like Brisbane, Newcastle, and Canberra are staggering compared to clubs like Easts, Souths, Norths, Balmain, St George, and my own. There are obviously too many clubs cluttering up the inner-city. Costs and drawing power will be the key to it.' Crowd figures for the 1988 season would seem to bear out Peter Moore's fears as, despite all-time attendance records of 1,690,073 for the Winfield Cup, almost 40 per cent of those fans supported the five teams outside Sydney.

Expansion, too, at national level, has been very much to the fore in Ken Arthurson's thinking. 'To compete with Australian Rules and soccer we had to put our game on a national basis. I was very worried that the code was played principally in only two states, and primarily in Sydney. Now with the new clubs, expansion in Western Australia where we have over eighty high school teams in competition and a league so strong that we are definitely considering setting up a professional club there within the next five years, and with development officers in every state, we have a healthy future. I am delighted that at last Australia can play a major part in international development.'

Ken Arthurson's promptings have had an effect and it is obvious that Australia's despatch of development officers of the quality of Peter Corcoran, Roy Masters, and John Lombie to the United States has been instrumental in much of the development there, especially at high school and university level. And their chairman intends to maintain the momentum.

The success of the Panasonic Cup match, between Parramatta and Balmain in March 1989 at the WACA ground in Perth, where over 24,000 spectators set up 'house full' notices, is proof of Ken Arthurson's vision of the future. 'We need more international teams playing Rugby League. We cannot exist in the future in a vacuum by ourselves. Australia intends to follow up progress in America with more help, both financial and human, and I also see Japan as a priority target. There is the money and interest among present Union players to develop Rugby League in the Far East.'

For too long Australia, basking in the strength of its domestic competitions, cushioned by the vast wealth generated by its clubs and magnificently successful on its limited international circuit has been negligent of its responsibilities for international expansion. It is heartening to see Ken Arthurson playing a major role in developing Rugby League outside the vast Australian continent. And he, I'm sure, would be only too ready to admit that international competition, as has happened in New Zealand, can cause an even greater surge of interest in the domestic game, and such a demand for Rugby League that if the potential is grasped, the code can prosper as never before.

The deeds of the Kiwi national coaches, Graham Lowe and Tony Gordon, and the successes of the teams under them in the 1980s certainly captured the imagination of a public whose staple diet in rugby had always been the gifted All Blacks Union side. Their success, allied to television exposure and constant media attention, had overshadowed the skills of New Zealand Rugby League; but once the Kiwis' Test successes against Great Britain and Australia in 1984 and 1986 had commanded similar media attention then the whole profile of the League code rose dramatically. Thankfully George Rainey, the president of the New Zealand Rugby League and chairman of their seven-man executive body, was ready to project the code in a positive manner. Though he and his executive members are busy looking after the eleven leagues scattered throughout the two islands of New Zealand, and stressing the values of youth rugby with the encouragement of a proliferation of Under-11 to Under-21 sides, he looks forward to even more hectic times in the near future. 'The game is outstripping the facilities which have suited us so well in the past sixty years. Because of the media interest and the resultant size of the crowds attracted to our games we need to find bigger and better stadiums. We need to widen the Rugby League public's horizons very quickly or we will lose the momentum that we have going for us.'

Those horizons are already being pushed back as Rainey's executive committee discusses the possibility of selling the famous Carlaw Park ground in Auckland, the home of New Zealand Test rugby, for industrial development. They envisage a new 40,000 all-seater stadium and office quarters being constructed out of the vast profits from such a sale. And, as interest in the League code rises, George Rainey foresees even more dramatic changes to the amateur ethos of New Zealand Rugby League. 'In five years, such is the strength of the code, Auckland will, I'm sure, have its first eight-club professional competition and Wellington and Canterbury will follow soon after'.

Such professional leagues would help to keep Kiwi stars like Shane Cooper, Kurt Sorenson, and Kevin Iro at home for a full domestic season instead of jetting about the world in search of financial reward for their talents. The professional leagues in those three cities would provide a huge incentive to players in the weaker country districts to improve their standards and promote themselves in the professional leagues. The system of pooling the receipts from all match attendances into a central fund for the promotion of Rugby League in Auckland, Christchurch, and Wellington will no doubt cease and the home club will be allowed to keep the receipts. Hence a revised system will allow the more adventurous clubs to prosper and attract even more revenue. Professional leagues would also attract even more sponsorship and encourage a greater awareness of Rugby League in industry, a trend which George Rainey welcomes. 'There would be good sponsorship backing for the clubs. The game in New Zealand is only just now learning to deal with sponsorship but already there are welcome signs that the game is a real attraction. Six years ago we had difficulty in finding a sponsor even for our national side; now, thanks to our success with Lion Red Breweries, sponsors are queuing up to join with us'. Like David Oxley and Ken Arthurson, George Rainey is confident that the expertise of his executive committee, the efforts of the Kiwi coach, Tony Gordon, and the charisma of the former coach, Graham Lowe, will continue to lift the code's image in New Zealand and exploit opportunities for future stars.

11

Full Circle

Whether Rugby League can adapt to the pressures and changing attitudes of society over the next twenty or thirty years must of course depend on its ability to compete with other team sports for players, media attention, spectators, and finance. Nothing attracts attention for a team sport like quality performance on the field and the pride stemming from international success at home and abroad. In this respect British Rugby League is making rapid headway and there are many youngsters coming into the game with considerable flair, talent, and dedication.

As we have seen, the outlook for both rugby codes in the state schools is grim. If we seek to raise the skill levels of our youngsters there can be no substitute for the practice of those skills under pressure in competitive matches. Moreover, if we are to continue to produce future international stars of the calibre of Mike Gregory, Shaun Edwards, or Andy Gregory, we must provide a competitive structure outside the schools as a complement to those schools which, thankfully, are still striving to maintain the quality of team competition. Both rugby codes in the struggle to attract youngsters have advantages peculiar to each but each has problems which must be overcome if either code is to flourish, albeit at the expense of the other.

Rugby Union will, I assume, continue to have a strong base in the public schools where it will often be the only winter sport played, and, like the old grammar schools, I believe that any new city technical school will ape the independent sector and choose Union as one of its winter sporting options. But that base is a very narrow one, especially in Wales, Scotland, and Ireland, and in my opinion is not strong enough or big enough to produce the quality of international recruits that it did in the past. Of course, Rugby Union still has a large network of state schools playing the game but it is a declining market and financially a burdensome one with little help from central funds. Rugby League has a smaller but concentrated area of schools in the north and is making significant advances in virgin territory in the Midlands and the south. But again, this base is far too narrow for comfort.

The League code's greatest strength, on the other hand, lies in the junior and primary schools where League, being a simpler game to play and involving more continuous handling and tackling for boisterous youngsters, has made rapid strides. Indeed, I would recommend the League game to all our Union-playing preparatory and independent junior schools as a means of developing the skills of running rugby and as a method of increasing the pupils' handling abilities. The introduction two years ago of Rugby League to Brighton College's junior school, an independent school, and the current good health of their teams who regularly travel to, and receive visitors from, as far afield as Leeds and St Helens, proves just what can be achieved. Here surely is one area for the London Rugby League development officer to explore.

Rugby League's biggest single advantage for the future is that, at long last, the stigma of playing League has been removed by the Union authorities themselves; and comprehensive education has in turn removed the once supposedly superior social advantage of playing Union in the old grammar schools. Even in the private school sector, where Leeds Grammar School and Ashville College, Harrogate played the first ever League fixture between independent schools in May 1989, the social barriers to Rugby League are breaking down. We now have a new generation of youngsters in the former grammar schools with no bias against the League code. Schools will, and must, play a part in Rugby League's future but before we look at the special part they will play it is worth noting that France plays neither Union nor League within the school curriculum nor as extra-curricular activity between schools, and yet, thanks to the liaison with clubs, they produce national schoolboy sides of considerable talent. We must learn a lesson from that.

France's major Rugby Union clubs are wealthy professional sporting organisations, able to offer important financial inducement to their best players, and are thus able to attract youngsters to the club. Rugby Union clubs in England do not have the same high profile or the same financial strength to help or in other ways impose themselves on local schools and their players as is done in France.

The idea of each Rugby Union club appointing liaison officers to assist schools and encourage schoolboys to link up with that club would have no greater impact than the old *ad hoc* system of a boy joining a club voluntarily when he finishes school. Most club liaison officers in Rugby Union are well meaning, eager men, but, as they are mostly unpaid and working in their spare time, their efforts hardly meet the needs of today. Other than a little correspondence between clubs and schools, usually pointing out the advantages of playing at the club, and the encouragement of an occasional coaching course, I see little profit from that sort of scheme. The appointment last season of a number of paid development officers, covering specific areas, should do much to help rectify the situation. But Union is looking after its own interests and making the best of the chaotic educational scene by putting its emphasis on youth rugby at club and representative level with Under-19 and Under-21 teams.

Though, admittedly, League has a much smaller base from which to develop its talents, it has much greater advantages in pursuing its work in schools and amateur clubs thanks to its professional nature. The many development officers in Rugby League are all full-time professional employees. Thus they can give all their time to the promotion of Rugby League and have the necessary funds at hand with which to do the job. While still encouraging the promotion of schoolboy teams, and town and inter-county competitions at all levels from Under-11s to Under-19s, the development officers take a realistic view of the future of schoolboy rugby.

Many development officers, alongside professional players, are working within a school's curriculum, and actually holding coaching sessions in school hours. Once the youngster has been encouraged to try his hand at the game and has developed a liking for it, he is then accommodated in one of the growing number of youth teams at his nearest amateur club. The rudiments and disciplines of the League code can thus be learned at school under the guidance of experts whilst the playing of the sport, if the school has no such facility, can be done at the local club. Such a concentration of hours and expertise from professional development officers and players, contracted by clubs, such as Wigan, Warrington, or Hull to perform these duties, can only broaden and strengthen Rugby League's base. It is heartening to see that many now realise just how narrow that base is by developing an awareness of the game in schools in Sheffield, Carlisle, Mansfield, and Hemel Hempstead – all areas completely or relatively new to the code.

The link between schools and amateur RL clubs can only help the clubs to prosper. With no discrimination now between the amateur sections of the two rugby codes, I forecast an even greater development of amateur League in once virgin territory. I really do see BARLA's dream of a League team operating in every major town or city being achieved by the time we reach Rugby League's centenary in 1995.

I am positive, too, that in the 1990s we will see the emergence of clubs and players playing both rugby codes. Financial problems will force many junior Rugby Union clubs to welcome League-playing sections to their premises as a means of increasing revenue over the bars and at functions. Such facilities will eventually be shared, with players playing the code of their preference at weekends or playing both, Union on a Saturday or League on a Sunday. Teams and clubs in Gloucester, Peterborough, Sedgemoor, Cheltenham, and Haringey have already pioneered such a system and the numbers of Gloucester Union players, men of the quality of Jim Breeze and Jeremy Bennett, first-team regulars, who took part in the Midlands and South-West Amateur RL Cup final in 1988 between Aberavon and Gloucester indicated the future trend. And why not? A few, as Mick Burke, David Stephenson and Shaun Edwards once achieved, at schoolboy level, may find themselves in the near future dual internationals at open-age amateur level.

Despite the heartening expansion of the professional game in the 1980s at Carlisle, Fulham, Mansfield, Chorley Borough and Trafford Borough there is now a greater need than ever to establish a national network of clubs. This task must be another priority for the Rugby Football League's board of directors and I do not feel the problem is as difficult as many would have us believe. We need to establish six or seven more professional or part-professional clubs over the next ten years and, though I am in complete agreement with David Oxley who insists that before any professional club is established there must be a history of strong amateur development, I believe the Rugby League's own insistence on high professional standards could actually stop us from grasping the opportunity to expand.

The need for impeccable standards in all the first division clubs is obvious since this division is the flagship of the code but I believe RL could learn a lesson from Rugby Union in its attempt at future growth. I would allow sides to enter my proposed third division as long as they were financially viable and able to afford a sprinkling of professional players. American Football has made a national impact by virtue of the names of the towns playing the sport – London, Nottingham, Fylde, Manchester, and Bristol – but, despite the overactive hype of certain sections of the media who would have us believe that the sport flourishes like no other, the clubs rarely play in front of more than 1500 people and some dip as low as 250. Yet it achieves a national presence and gains a media interest which the small number of clubs, players, and spectators taking part really does not warrant.

Rugby Union, too, achieves a similar and greater impact by virtue of its spread of localities. A mere handful of spectators, often only parents, wives or girl-friends, will watch Old Reigatians in Surrey, Blaydon in the North-East or Ruskin Park but their presence in the mainstream of the Union code is vital. League must try to do the same. Professional teams are the main marketing product of the League code no matter how strong and successful amateur development may be and, if a sport cannot command the attention of a capital city like London then it will always have a problem. There should be two or three professional clubs in London, two based in the south-west, where there is a natural interest in rugby; two in the Midlands, where Mansfield have bravely shown what can be achieved with hard work; one in the north-east, an area which once boasted a club in Newcastle; and possibly a further venture in Wales, perhaps based in Aberavon where amateur League has aroused considerable interest. 'A flight of fancy', I hear some say, but I believe that such clubs can be formed over the next ten years. We are not looking in the early years for 10,000 crowds, superstars playing in the teams, or even gaining honours, but like Rugby Union and American Football we need to win an awareness of Rugby League at national level in the minds of the public, potential sponsors, and the media.

I welcome the RFL's plans to create a merchandising business, operating from headquarters in Leeds with its own sales force. A merchandising section should generate considerable income from the vigorous marketing and licensing of Rugby League products through mail order, chain stores, and the code's own retail outlets.

The huge injection of sponsorship money, over £3m in 1988–89 from national companies, such as Bass, British Coal, John Player, Whitbread and NORWEB, has, of course, been warmly welcomed by the RFL but the sponsors in turn have welcomed the style of play of our national and top professional sides and have been glad to lend their brand name to a relatively trouble free, fast, tough, lively game. Such is the pace and vigour of the game today that I foresee few major law changes in the 1990s. Perhaps we may see tinkerings with the scrummage laws (oh, that a hooker, as in Union, were made to pack with his feet in a pushing position). But I doubt if there will be any major changes.

So far as Rugby Union is concerned, having held up its hands in horror for over ninety years at the thought of organised leagues, the Rugby Union authorities now see such a structure as the saviour of the code's international reputation. No less a person than John Burgess, a recent president of the RFU, declared in their defence, 'From the Rugby Football Union's point of view it was gratifying to see leagues welcomed with such enthusiasm in most parts of the country and at virtually every level of the game.' Such a noted defender of the amateur ethos and of the original concepts of the Rugby Union code might have cause to regret their introduction.

Leagues will provide competitive Rugby Union but, unlike Rugby League, they may not necessarily provide exciting and spectacular rugby. It is impossible to play negatively in Rugby League since the modern laws place all the emphasis on attack and, since the removal of the unlimited-tackle law, it is now impossible for a side merely to win a match by denying the opposition the ball. Not so in Rugby Union, where I am afraid I have seen far too many league matches which have resulted in nine- or ten-man rugby with the half-back moving the ball up and down the touchlines with his kicking boot. Such tactics are too easy; and the influence of the pack and set-piece play has become much too important.

Crowds at Rugby Union matches may have increased considerably at Bath, Bristol, and Gloucester and the media awareness and national consciousness of Union may have increased out of all proportion to its spectator interest at, say, Waterloo or Liverpool/St Helens. Leagues may be producing the competitive edge and the forward aggression which allowed England's pack to dictate terms to the Irish in last season's Five Nations championship but in terms of producing exhilarating, attacking rugby with the scoring of tries as the main priority, I fear it will not. The constraints of Rugby Union's laws determine the style of play when their league clubs battle for points. Martin Johnson, in his report of the Nottingham v.

Leicester Courage League match of last season in the *Independent*, accurately sums up my feelings: 'The Courage League is something of a misnomer, in that it is largely about fear. Give it everything, but risk nothing, with legs and lungs engaged at full throttle, and matches between the forwards that could be comfortably accommodated in a telephone kiosk. A chronic case for Agoraphobics Anonymous.'

But, whatever kind of game evolves, the leagues in Union have, I believe, already begun to change the complexion of the game and have made serious inroads into the code's amateur concept. Let me state from the outset that, having been a professional Rugby League player myself, I have nothing whatever against the possibility of professional Union players. I merely assess the situation in the light of the hypocritical stance of many leading Union administrators and players who cover up any payments they may receive and yet cast a slight on the 13-a-side game. Indeed Steve Smith, the former England Union captain, best summed up the current situation in this country, where many Union players are paid 'liberal expenses' when, at a dinner I attended with him, he declared, 'The only difference between League and Union players is that League players pay tax.'

It has now become fashionable for players, coaches, and some administrators to advocate the introduction of Trust funds for Rugby Union players, a system by which, as in athletics, the money earned by players from books they have written, their endorsement of products, advertising, and guest appearances here and there would be paid into a fund to be made available on their retirement. A significant number of leading figures in the Union world, notably Will Carling, the current England captain, Geoff Cooke, his coach, and Ray Williams, the former secretary of the Welsh RFU have supported such a devious payment scheme. Queensland players have proposed a similar scheme while Brian Thomas, Neath's one-time manager, actually proposes a return to what almost amounts to broken-time payments for his players, many of whom are farmers and who, when they are away on training sessions with the Welsh Rugby Union, 'have to fork out money to get their work done'. Tom Hudson, a much respected coach at Bath and a man whose work and attitude I greatly admire, offers a suggestion to stop players taking the path to Rugby League. He says, 'I am not saying players should be paid for playing rugby but I think we'll have to sit down and work out how Trust funds might work; but I'd want it to operate for players in need'.

Gentlemen, who are we fooling? Why be such hypocrites? The Trust fund or any other device for rewarding Union players with money is merely a confidence trick to try to establish the so-called moral ascendancy that Victorian gentlemen who played Union once thought they had over their semi-professional counterparts in Rugby League. What different is there in a pay packet at the end of every week to a bumper pay-out at the end of your career? Talk of Trust funds is just another attempt to paint the Union player as whiter than white at the expense of the professional League player who earns his money openly.

I have more respect for the secretary of the RFU, Dudley Wood, who honestly and sincerely expressed his views when talk about Trust funds became the fashion. There was no hypocrisy or cant from him but a statement of true amateur views, which are worthy of respect. 'A Trust fund or deferred-payment scheme is little more than a contrived arrangement to circumvent amateur regulations, an artificial device which enables a professional to call himself an amateur,' said Wood. The IB's regulations relating to amateurism are quite clear on this point: no person may accept the promise of future payment or benefit or other material reward for taking part in the game. This regulation has the unreserved support of the RFU.

Already players are on the move from club to club in search of even more 'liberal expenses' and, in the north, Union club scouts are now rivalling even the League scouts in their keenness to attract recruits to a club. I find the situation a most intriguing one as Union is learning to cope with a situation which has come full circle since that historic breakaway by League, or the Northern Union as it was then called. Rugby League learns to cope with a sudden upsurge of interest in the code at amateur level while Union is forced to come to terms with, and perhaps adjust its principles to, professionalism.

Payments are already being made to players at Union clubs in Britain. At the beginning of the 1988–89 season in England we had the bizarre situation of the RFU secretary, Dudley Wood, setting up a task force to ensure that the game's amateur laws were being obeyed. He promised that the 'amateurism sub-committee will pay unannounced visits to ensure that clubs are keeping proper accounts and that players' expenses are within the rules'. Few club treasurers trembled at his threat. And in Wales an exit of players from the Aberavon club was brought about by their complaints that players at the club did not receive the same perks as other players at other clubs in Wales. They were in effect losing out in a competitive market.

I foresee a system whereby a Union club might pay 'liberal expenses' to attract a couple of internationals while other players in the club remain pure amateurs. The problem for the Union is that, as I have already overheard in a couple of northern clubs, once players are given financial handouts then the coaches, physiotherapists, bar staff, and groundsmen seek payment too. The cry goes up,

'Why should I work for nothing five nights a week when a player is getting paid?' However, I am sure the appointment of Barrie Corless, the former England Rugby Union international, as Northampton's full-time administrator, in effect the Union code's first professional club manager, is one that will escalate. Indeed, the Norwich Rugby Union club, hardly one of Britain's leading clubs, languishing in the Courage London League (second division north) at the end of the 1988–89 season, advertised for a coach-cum-player-cum-administrator at a salary of between £15–20,000 a year. Not bad – but surely the first step towards the payment of the playing staff.

Incidentally, I find it altogether puzzling that players selected for a British Amateur Rugby League tour of Australasia are required to find at least £300 themselves before they can join the party. At the same time the Rugby Union International Board of Control in the spring of 1989 raised the weekly allowance for the British Lions party to £126, despite the fact that food and accommodation was being paid in full. Please reflect: which player is the true amateur?

A second problem for Rugby Union, in the drift to professionalism, is the fact that outside the Midlands and the south-west, spectator interest at club level is simply not enough to sustain any form of professionalism, especially not in London and the north. Major clubs like Waterloo, Liverpool/St Helens, Headingley, and Sale can barely attract 1000 spectators for even their best fixtures and often have gates which drop as low as 300–500. By comparison, Rugby League clubs in towns and cities such as St Helens, Wigan and Leeds can attract crowds from 10,000–20,000, yet still have problems balancing their accounts. Professionalism will present more problems to Union than even its most ardent supporters can imagine.

Sadly for Rugby Union in Britain its standards are

slipping when compared to the might of South Africa, New Zealand, and France, where professionalism is rampant. South Africa threatens to stage its own professional circus of Union players in an attempt to make good the lack of international competition brought about by other countries' revulsion at its apartheid policies. Indeed, I was even approached by a South African contact in January 1989 to see whether I would be prepared to manage a joint League/Union squad of professional players to tour South Africa the following summer or autumn. Jonathan Davies was also asked if he would be available to play under my managership.

Louis Luyt, the president of Transvaal Rugby Union, has millions of pounds at his disposal and the support of large companies ready to take advantage of the South African government's 65 per cent tax rebate for sports sponsorship. New Zealand allowed many of their Cavaliers team, who had taken part in a pirate tour of South Africa the previous year, to play in the inaugural World Cup of 1987. It is more than significant that New Zealand refused to impose the International Board's ruling that twelve weeks must elapse before a player, following the last match of his domestic season, can play rugby overseas. Such a ruling, obviously intended to stop Kiwis, Australians and South Africans from earning considerable sums of money by playing off-season in Italy and France, has been totally ignored in order to alleviate the pressures of professionalism. In France, despite television exposure of how many francs change hands at leading Union clubs, professional practices continue and even make Rugby League clubs suffer since they are unable to offer similar attractive payments to their potential recruits.

France's former full-back and captain, Pierre Villepreux, caused a furore when he readily confessed to being paid to coach the Toulouse Union team and revealed that all his players are, like himself, full professionals. 'I am paid as much as my players but no more. People at the Federation are aware of it.' Rugby Union in France is played in an attractive style, with the emphasis on scoring tries and with entertainers like their full-back, Serge Blanco, given full scope to display his running skills. Such an attitude is a professional one, brought about by professional players having the time to practise and train, often during the day when English players are working, and by the necessity to entertain large crowds. As with Rugby League clubs, so with French Union clubs, if large gate revenues are to be generated then they must play in an entertaining way to attract the spectators and win friends through television.

If Rugby Union players in Britain cannot afford the unlimited time for skill training, fitness work, and weight training that their overseas counterparts can, or as can their Rugby League colleagues, then their standards must inevitably decline. Here then lies the dilemma for Rugby Union for, if it seeks to catch up with the leading Union playing countries, it must, whether it likes it or not, turn professional.

Finance will bring the two rival codes in Britain much closer together. As payments in the major Union clubs become more important, the Union code, as League realised by the early 1900s, will need to attract ever larger numbers of spectators at club level to finance their operations. And, like Rugby League, the Union authorities will find that they will have to simplify their game, very much in the way that Rugby League has done. If, eventually, payments to certain players become an open and accepted part of Rugby Union policy then what is to stop the interchange of star players at international level?

By the time we approach the year 2000, I foresee another problem which could bring the two codes together – the need for competition between the leading clubs of either code. As I have already indicated, no northern club can generate the spectator interest or funds necessary to meet the professional demands of leading Rugby Union players today. And Rugby League is now so strongly entrenched in the north that many Union stars will always transfer allegiance for cash while vast numbers of youngsters, once accustomed to move into Union, are now playing amateur League or are being snapped up by the professional clubs. I cannot foresee a time in the near future when the counties of Yorkshire, Lancashire, and Cumbria will ever again dominate the Rugby Union world. It is significant that the schools that once produced such England internationals as Tony Neary, Roger Uttley, John Carleton, John Horton, Kevin Simms, Pat Quinn and Reg Higgins have either disappeared or are introducing their youngsters to Rugby League. It is again not without significance that only one northern team, Wakefield, figured in the last eight of the Pilkington Cup during the 1988–89 season and that both Waterloo and Liverpool/St Helens struggled all season to keep even a toehold on the first division of the Courage League.

Such will be the limitations of a northern Union club in future that we may soon see an elite body of clubs in the south-east and south-west, straddling the M4, rather like the League clubs now sitting astride the M62. Only Bath, Bristol, Leicester, Wasps and Harlequins are likely to be able to generate sufficient funds through gate receipts or through private benefactors and sponsorship to keep their players content and themselves able to recruit the best Union talent.

No club outside London and the south-west can generate a sponsorship deal of over £100,000 as Harlequins have done for the next three years with Red Star Parcels; and so they will fail to attract the top players who may then decide to go south or, if they are good enough, will start to play Rugby League.

There will be an equally wide gulf between northern and southern Rugby Union clubs as there is between the rival codes. Surely, at some time, the might of the Union code along the M4 will have little competition other than with the strongholds alongside the M62. Hypothetical, true, but a scenario that is already developing. Do we then see a coming together of the two codes and a healing of the great split of 1895? It is extremely doubtful in the near future but certainly both codes of rugby will be forced to accommodate each other in a way that they have never had to do before. In the more distant future I would not be too surprised to see the rivals come together on the field of play, perhaps first in the form of challenge matches between the two codes as in the war-time internationals played at Bradford and Leeds, and then later, perhaps, as one game, the outcome of the best of both codes.

In any event, whatever happens, whatever the future for the oval ball, I have no doubt that it will continue to give pleasure to countless thousands. Hopefully, whatever code they play, coach, or commentate upon they will receive as much satisfaction as I have done from my involvement with the greatest game of all – rugby.